55 *Reflections* of a *Searching Skeptic*

*Explore the Faith Journey of a
Poetic Bipolar Believer*

by Rich Melcher
Foreword by Rosemary Murphy, Ph.D.

Copyright © 2023 Rich Melcher.

All rights reserved. No part of this book may be reproduced, stored, or transmitted by any means—whether auditory, graphic, mechanical, or electronic—without written permission of both publisher and author, except in the case of brief excerpts used in critical articles and reviews. Unauthorized reproduction of any part of this work is illegal and is punishable by law.

"The Scripture citations used in this work are taken from the Saint Joseph Edition of the New American Bible, revised edition, copyright (c) 2011, by Catholic Book Publishing Corporation, New Jersey."

Library of Congress Control Number: 2019906158
ISBN: 979-8-88640-684-9 (sc)
ISBN: 979-8-88640-685-6 (hc)
ISBN: 979-8-88640-686-3 (e)

Because of the dynamic nature of the Internet, any web addresses or links contained in this book may have changed
since publication and may no longer be valid. The views expressed in this work
are solely those of the author and do not necessarily reflect the views of the
publisher, and the publisher hereby disclaims any responsibility for them.

One Galleria Blvd., Suite 1900, Metairie, LA 70001
1-888-421-2397

*This book is dedicated to my dad,
who showed me how
to become a man of significance.*

CONTENTS

Foreword vii
Preface ix
Introduction xi

Reflections . . .
1. Other sheep 1
2. Worthy of the call 5
3. The Skeptic 7
4. Two readings on the Transfiguration of Jesus Christ 10
5. The turn around 11
6. Me, bipolar?...a look at Crisis '80 14
7. Poor in spirit 19
8. Laughter 22
9. Jesus cures the leper 23
10. Jesus found safe in the temple 24
11. Called me by name 25
12. Charisms 27
13. Humility 31
14. Peaceful Prayer in the deserted places 33
15. Integrity bubbling up 35
16. A Fool on Fire 37
17. Paying patience 53
18. Say "YES!!!" 55
19. Saved by Corsair 57
20. The RROCKSS CODE 59
21. Give it away 73
22. Importance of PLACE 75
23. Enough! 77
24. if I told you 78
25. and with fire 80
26. Sign of the Cross 82
27. Fully Human 84
28. Evangelization 86
29. Remnants 88
30. Oil & Vinegar 90
31. Childlike Faith 92

32. "No hurries, no worries" 93
33. Whoever believes 95
34. The REAL Birthday 97
35. Love is patient 99
36. Jesus & me 100
37. Getting into the real 105
38. Multitasking 108
39. Love one another 109
40. a multi-blessing 111
41. You act black! 113
42. The woman at the well 119
43. Easter Reflections 120
44. The tassel 122
45. Freedom From 124
46. Joy and Peace 126
47. Anger! 127
48. Beyond the distressing disguise 130
49. Feel 131
50. 2 journal entries 133
51. Something constructive to do 138
52. Jesus looked at the heart 140
53. End meets the beginning 142
54. Loose cannon blues 144
55. Butterfly blind spot 146
56. P.S. 148
57. P.P.S. 152

About the Author 155

FOREWORD

55 Reflections of a Searching Skeptic

Inspirational writers often use images of a journey to make the point that we are not solo travelers on the road of life. Often in sharing life experiences with their fellow travelers—the joyous and the challenging—human beings find a unique oneness and their deepest connection with others.

The experience of not traveling alone is the sentiment that pervades author and poet, Rich Melcher's highly personal journey, *55 Reflections of a Searching Skeptic*. He opens a path and welcomes the reader to join him in a series of spiritual reflections. Therefore it is helpful for the reader to approach Melcher's work as a spiritual companion. To be a companion to Melcher, one must slow down, quiet down and be willing to ponder the twists and turns, the ups and downs of one man's revelations about the spiritual life.

Reflection is not a linear experience and neither is the content of Melcher's book. To fully appreciate the value of his work, one has to suspend literary judgments and enter into the spirit of the narration and poetry. If the reader meets Rich Melcher as a person who walks every day with the chronic challenges of bipolar disorder, one can begin to appreciate the connection between deep mental suffering and the heightened creativity that can be its grace.

The reflections shared by a "searching skeptic" involve the reader and encourage his or her compassion. Even if the reader knows little about mental illness, or even if one has lived with and cared for someone who has bipolar disorder or even if, in fact, the reader has bipolar, Melcher's shared experiences are spiritually compelling, especially when he writes about his illness and the benefits of the medications, counseling, and self-talk it takes to stay the journey when one realizes that bipolar will be a life-long companion.

In 2008, Rich Melcher legally adopted the name of a World War II fighter plane "Corsair," as a moniker for the positive, energetic power that is his protective and freeing interior force. His new middle name functions on several levels of meaning. Rich Corsair Melcher himself becomes a metaphor for the lifting up of the human spirit "when hope runs thin." Mental illness, physical in nature, can be a terrifying inner disturbance—a deep sadness of the soul. By publicly taking on a symbol of something that uplifts (Corsair) and releases some of the sadness, Melcher was able to begin writing—his life-long avocation.

55 Reflections of a Searching Skeptic, part personal narrative and part poetry, is a treasure. Melcher's journey is not finished, however. He is still overcoming the obstacles of putting to rest "my suffered self" and discovering "the soothing voice of interior silence." When he became self-aware of his journey which he shares so intimately with the reader, his life was changed and he was filled "with a joy I hadn't felt in months, if not years! It was all worth it! It was the way it was supposed to be!"

Enjoy traveling with Corsair. Be uplifted and find hope in sharing another man's journey.

Rosemary Murphy, Ph.D., Milwaukee, Wisconsin, April 1, 2019

PREFACE

Sometimes life doesn't make any sense. Some try to make sense of it and often fail. I claim to make no sense of it, only to offer a few words of encouragement and insight that have branched out of me, and now onto you.

This is a conversational, journal-style, reflection-oriented, somewhat autobiographical book. It often reads more like a conversation than a self-help, non-fiction or text book, and borders on a spiritual-reading book. It is meant to spark deeper thought and important conversations. But, basically, it is meant to chronical my spiritual walk of thought, prayer and personal experiences. I hope you enjoy the walk.

The name CORSAIR is my pen name and also my acquired middle name, which will be described later in the book.

I hope this book brings you many new insights and ideas to think and pray about.

Corsair, Rich Melcher, a joyful, grateful, searching skeptic

INTRODUCTION

"To thine own self be true, and thou canst not be false to any man" is a quote from Shakespeare's *Hamlet* that I have been hearing a lot lately. A year or two ago, I scribed 60 meaningful quotes, in permanent ink, on the surface of a volley ball, which I call the "Wisdom Ball". The ball I use for recovery groups at mental health venues where I work. You toss the ball up, and where the right thumb lands on a quote, the participant reads it aloud and is encouraged to comment on it—a few words or many—whatever comes to mind. Others can then comment too.

Three times recently this "To thine own self be true" quote has attracted clients' thumbs, and clear voices have commented:

> *"I think this is really true. Being true to yourself is really important"* or

> *"What does 'thine' mean?"* or

> *"Yeah, this really fits me right now. I struggle with my alcoholism every day! Just craving that next drink puts my 3-day sobriety at risk. But I gotta stay away. I can't go back. It will kill me. 'To thine own self be true'—that's something I really needed to hear today!"*

The *Wisdom Ball* brings self-reflection, enlightenment, and a way for people to get to know one another—and themselves.

Then, playing *Wisdom Ball* once again, my thumb touched the same quote, and it occurred to me that this was something I needed to pay attention to. I had written down the quote from Shakespeare's Hamlet when I enjoyed my nephew, as a high school senior, play the lead role in the play in the 1990s. It rang true to me then, as it did again during recovery group.

Just as I was contemplating the notion of writing this, *my next book* (something I have been yearning to write for years), this quote appeared in my life again—**BE TRUE, BE TRUE**—and I was inspired to begin writing, and inserting previous writings and poetry, to create this book.

But there was one thing…**"How 'BE TRUE' do I dare to get?"** What follows is the first of 55 reflections as I respond to that question.

REFLECTION 1

OTHER SHEEP

"Jesus said to him, 'I am the way and the truth and the life. No one comes to the Father except through me.'" (John 14:6). There are a few Bible verses I have put to memory—this is one. There was a time, some 20-25 years ago (or before), when I heard this quote of John's Gospel as comforting and reassuring. Then, somewhere in my spiritual walk—possibly around the age of 40—it came to me in a new, disturbing way:

"I am the way and the truth and the life.
*NO ONE COMES TO THE FATHER **EXCEPT** **THROUGH** **ME**!"*

For me, John had regressed in my spiritual trust, and I saw that I had been living a mistruth. As soon as I married my first wife, in 1998, I sluffed off all remnants of my Catholic faith practices and followed her to her "happy-happy" non-denominational church near the home we had bought in suburban Minneapolis.

In that marriage, I became a non-assertive, acquiescing, follow-along **sheep**, led by a kind, outgoing, gregarious, benignly-overbearing woman who shepherded me right out of a previous life as a Catholic, and into a comfortable, welcoming, enlivening "happy happy" church. There was no creed, no rituals of consequence or sacraments, as in the Catholic Church. It preached "the happy" through soothing, but thought-provoking, heart-felt sermons on a stage with the congregation sitting in folding chairs.

To be real, I had been attending an *enlivening, social justice-oriented Catholic church* near downtown Minneapolis for years before our marriage, and had loved the atmosphere, the people, the Mass structure and the rituals. But all this had been stripped away by my weak decision to bah-bah break away from my past spiritual life, all for the sake of fitting in. (To thine own self be true?). I believe this is when skepticism truly arose in me. And I am a skeptic to this day—but a *searching* skeptic.

Oh, I found a writing of mine from 2001:

W, T & L
Way, Truth and Life

If you blindly believe in an idea
You may be missing the reality

the focus on "I am the way
and the truth and the life" is not
the "no one can come to the Father
except through me"
*but that **THE WAY** who*
Jesus was (is)—to me—
that I focus on His personal
and divine attributes . . .

faith, hope, love,
mercy, courage, humility,
forgiveness, compassion, wisdom,
perseverance, honesty, generosity,
hospitality, patience, gratitude . . .

Jesus lived an abundant life
when He walked His paths
on Earth…I believe
*His **WAY** was the*
cumulative effect of His
attributes . . .

(I guess I had some insight even back in 2001!)

I've dogged and even despised the Apostle John for his exclusivity for years, tired of his "John 3:16," and his long-winded, theological exposés/commentaries on Jesus' doings, thick with quotes attributed to Jesus, as if anyone—especially a man of simple stories and parables—would speak like that! (Yes, I am taking the risk of blasphemous questioning of the sacred Scripture, but this is how I see it). I have suffered with the "It must be true—it's in the Bible"- syndrome, at one time coming to the knowing that, yes, it was inspired by God, but written by old, white Jewish men who had their own slants, agendas and audiences, speaking and writing about the life of Christ. With translation upon translation, Jesus' original words, in my view, probably got somewhat skewed—or at least sounded much different.

Then, in April of this year, 2018, the Sunday Gospel, (at the African American Catholic church I now am a member of, All Saints, in Milwaukee, Wisconsin), offered this simple Gospel reading:

*". . . I have other sheep that do not belong to this fold.
These also I must lead, and they will hear my voice,
and there will be one flock, one shepherd."
John 10:16*

I was flabbergasted! "This was John? My ol' buddy JOHN? How could it be? This was INCLUSIVE!!"

I scribbled down the citation, John 10:16, in the mini notebook I carry with me everywhere I go and looked it up in my Bible when I got home from Mass. Sure enough, what I had heard was what it read! **"I have other sheep who do not belong to this fold."** Inspired by its inclusivity, I wrote page after page in my journal, enlarging and printing off a copy of the citation to tape alongside my journal entries.

Then, later that week, my favorite uncle died, and I headed to Forsyth, Montana, where Uncle JD was from, and reunited with four of my brothers and two of my sisters, as we gathered for the funeral.

Although the reunion with my siblings was joyful, I had mixed feelings about our encounters. On one hand, it was great to see them again and share a few pleasant meals before and after the funeral. But, on the other hand, I found myself "being my old self"—not speaking much—spectating rather than participating — yet authentically laughing when the laugh-lines came. I was there but not there—not willing or able to keep up with their gregarious small talk, entering into beer-tasting moments, or recanting of old family stories.

I wanted to hear and share stories of our recent struggles and triumphs, to discuss "deeper" social topics and to get to know them better on a more personal level. But that was certainly not the direction they were going. I'm not blaming—only explaining. My reaction was not their fault; it was just the old "gathering with the Melchers" pattern playing out like a broken record in my mind. My unwelcomed melancholic temperament was getting the best of me.

But God had something in store for me (and them) that I didn't see coming. Without any pressing expectations, I got together with my four brothers, individually, during the two days in Montana, and comfortably but excitedly shared with them about the John 10:16 reading and how it affected me, and wondering how it would affect them. Each time, we entered into a reflective, reverent, spiritual space—seemingly with them knowing this was where they could truly reach ME, and I could touch them.

It was a blessing—blessing upon blessing! When I got home to Milwaukee, I almost immediately gravitated toward my computer and began tapping out my ideas and observations—my soul:

Other Sheep

In the Gospel reading from Sunday, April 22, Earth Day, it was fitting that Jesus spoke of the Good Shepherd, a universal theme. One verse rang true in my ears (I had been searching for it for many years)…

John 10:16......"I have other sheep that do not belong to this fold. These also I will lead, and they will hear my voice, and there will be one flock, one shepherd...."

For over a dozen years I have struggled with the presence of "exclusion" in, most predominantly, the Gospel of John, in statements like, "I am the way, the truth and the life. No one comes to the father EXCEPT THROUGH ME." (!!!) I had seen where Jesus was very inclusive (ministering to the Gentiles, the woman at the well or with blind Bartimaeus), but I could not get these exclusive verses out of my consciousness—Way, Truth & Life—until two Sundays ago.

*Ironically, it was the words of John that broke the glass church ceiling. This made it all the more powerful. I heard Jesus saying, "<u>I accept everyone</u> into my Kingdom—Jews, Muslims, Hindus, Buddhists; all religions, the unchurched, the unbelievers, the agnostics—everyone! Sure, Christians may have a special place in my heart, but **everyone** is welcome, whether they believe in me or not."*

This one verse freed me up inside. Walls of doubt and skepticism came crashing down. And to know it was from one of the four Gospels—it holds a lot of weight. It wasn't just Habakkuk or Sirach—it was John!

It is also ironic that the reading came on Earth Day, April 22, a day for Jesus to tell the whole Earth that, no matter their belief, or nonbelief (or anywhere in between), they are accepted by Him in His Love. With contradictions such as this in John, the Bible is, as I see it, a strange, confusing, wonderful place!

by Corsair, Rich Melcher

This reading wasn't forced; I didn't coax an audience; it just came from my mind and heart. Excited to share this expression of my authentic self, I emailed it to my brothers and sisters from the Montana trip, to the rest of my immediate family, and to a few close friends, in the joy of discovery and Grace.

Almost immediately I received an email back from my oldest sister, who was at the Montana gathering. I was surprised to hear that, although I perceived her as a "non-believer," she said that this is what she believed all along! God touched me with insight, and it allowed me to touch her. It was a completely unexpected and beautiful moment!

Maybe a skeptic can be redeemed . . . through being genuine, listening to a call, and assertively acting upon it.

REFLECTION 2
Worthy of the call

> "I (Paul), then, a prisoner for the Lord, urge you to live in a manner
> worthy of the call you have received, with all humility and gentleness,
> with patience, bearing with one another through love,
> striving to preserve the unity of the spirit through
> the bond of peace.…" Ephesians 4: 1-3

Hey, that's assuming you have a call or even know what the call is! Paul's "prison" seems, to me, to have been **to write**. When you see a statue of Paul, he is often brandishing a two-edged sword—the sword of the Word, the Word of God, that he had been called to wield. This was the burden that got him put into prison (numerous times), ship wrecked, beaten, scourged and nearly stoned to death, (think of the PTSD this guy must have had!). Yet he felt he was called—*to write*. **It was his *charism*.**

Sure he occasionally went on and on in somewhat incomprehensibly long sentences, but just think of the pressure. He was a man of NOW and he never knew when or where his enemies were going to catch up with him next (he was probably an "eat your dessert first" kind of guy). He was emblazed with THE RESPONSIBILITY to not only write but create the content, through the workings of the Holy Spirit, of course. But still, he was the one energized, and burdened, to stay up nights and get up early mornings, always thinking of the next letter he was going to write—his next proclamation. I wonder how he wrote all of those letters from prison. Was it like Dr. Martin Luther King, Jr., writing messages on little scraps of paper, never dreaming it would become *the letter from the Birmingham jail*?

And this "call thing" Paul wrote about…how do we know we have a calling? Does our calling come from our education, our job, our after-hour activities, our kids, our phone conversations? What is it, you may be wondering?!

Funny, it was just a few days ago that I truly realized what may be my call. Like Paul, it has been made clear to me that my calling also is to write. Give me a cocktail party and I am so ill-at-ease that I could crawl behind the bar. But give me a cocktail party napkin to scribble down an insightful thought or new idea for a piece I am writing, and I feel fulfilled!

I want to write what I hear in my heart—and let the mind do the editing. It is my calling. And I am very excited to get on with it!

calling

> *Mark 12: 30-31*
> *"... and you shall love*
> *the Lord, your God, with all your heart,*
> *with all your soul, with all your mind,*
> *and with all your strength,*
> *and love your neighbor as yourself."*

and so it is written
this is the call
this is the rally cry
for our hearts and minds
to divorce themselves from the insanity
of this modern day's tensions
and the ever-present dangers
that hold them at knife-point

it seems so simple
to LOVE and cherish one another
in the daylight and twilight
as brothers and sisters

yet it seems almost too daunting
that we are called to this Love
with all we are—no holding back
no regretting what might have been ours

had we clenched our fists
around the currency of safety and security
and hoped others would have just left us alone
could we really have spent our lives
in a solemn solitude of the mind?

no—God has something else planned
that we reach out
that we caress and comfort
at the expense of our pride
and ease of connectedness

this is our calling—to LOVE
this is God's plea
will you hear it?
will you adhere to it?

Corsair

REFLECTION 3
THE SKEPTIC

Certainty is not the aim. Clarity is. Absolutism is not the goal. Curiosity is. Dogma is not the rule. Observation is. Skepticism does not mean you don't believe; it means you may not have all the evidence or heart-assuredness to make a conclusive decision.

I am a self-proclaimed skeptic. No one has ever pegged me as such, but I know my heart. And often my heart says "WAIT!" Wait for that next inspiration. Wait for that next piece of information because it might be the one that steers me into certainty—and certainty would be nice.

But more than "nice," I am looking for Truth and growth and a vision that will shine through the hazy patches into the light of KNOWING. If I make my decision too soon, I may be lost in the fog of others' opinions and viewpoints. Killer, for me!

Sometimes skepticism comes in unlikely packages—the Bible, to name one. I have so many questions about how and why and for whom it was written that I can get mired in the details, and waver in my belief that this all actually happened. "How could a boat carry every species of Guinea pig, much less African <u>and</u> Indian elephants—and all the rest of the hundreds of thousands of species of birds and fauna? The "boat" would have to be about the size of Delaware!" My disbelief can carry on and on.

(2013 journal entry follows):

> Faith: is it a gift or an achievement?
>
> If faith is a gift, receiving it is merely the beginning. We need also to recognize it, understand it and utilize it; then give thanks for it.
>
> Often, such as now, I feel faith is an achievement. I am struggling to find and grasp it in my own life. It's as though I have to earn it, through study, activities, contemplation and countering questionable beliefs that surround me in my everyday Christian world. It gets tiring, frustrating, discouraging. I want a solution, but, over the past 30 years, similar gnawing questions remain.

But somehow, I try to make sense of the world around me. I remember the musical group, the *Talking Heads*' plea to "Stop Making Sense" and how freeing that can be! Life is all too much of a jumble to make sense of. Yet there must be some order or it all goes hay wire.

So I do my best to follow my heart, and stay in touch with what I DO believe. In the end, I think, though, that I will always have the heart of a skeptic. Not good, not bad, just a little unsure.

The Skeptic

never believing
on first face value
deer in the headlights
dodging the oncoming flash
dashing into ditches

then becomes rabbit
curious beyond first view
dried leaves rustling in the gutter
presumed threat enough

*to hide and gaze
amid the tall grasses*

*more info creates the cautious puppy
leaning on instinct to guide
approaching the situation strongly
gladly, curiously*

*and finally the skeptic
becomes a man or woman
ready to meet and stare down
the details while observing
all the subtleties and nuances
to make sure the scene is valid
and secure and understandable*

*only then can a skeptic become
a believer
(maybe)*

Corsair

REFLECTION 4

Two readings on the Transfiguration of Jesus Christ . . .

I had prayed before going out cross-country skiing this afternoon to be blessed with the grace to see the gospel choir I sing in in a new way. I belong to a Catholic gospel choir and sing in the bass section. I used to be a tenor but was switched because we had 12 tenors and 2 basses. The basses needed numbers and volume, not necessarily talent. Thing is, my voice range is in between the two—I can't sing the higher tenor notes nor the lower bass notes. So I don't really fit in either section well.

While praying about *the Transfiguration* of Jesus on the mountain—as I skied, God brought me to that new place. I was imagining Moses and Elijah standing by Jesus, emblazed in white, but wondered how Peter, James and John could know who they were—since they had never met them before, <u>and</u> their view was skewed by the brilliant white light. I imagined Moses holding two large stone tablets and Elijah holding a large book—the Old Testament.

Then, out of the blue, I came to realize that my choir practices were actually *prayer meetings*. Like seeing Jesus myself in flashy whiteness, I saw the light that I was to praise God at choir practice and not think of them as practices or to be consumed by which notes I could hit or not. I was awakened to see it as worship-time. Funny how God inspires us at the oddest times—skiing! I was *transfigured* in heart and mind. Choir became a multi-blessing, in the blink of an eye!

A few weeks ago, as we acknowledged Jesus' Transfiguration in Mass, we were blessed to have Fr. Scott from Sacred Heart School of Theology as celebrant. His homily was about how often we are disfigured by our sin, by the trials we encounter, by troubles caused by addictions.

"Disfigurement" often involves the face, and today I witnessed discouraging facial disfigurement. I went to a shoe store to buy a pair of tennies, and both sales clerks "greeted me" with glum faces. No smiles. No "do you like those shoes?" Just deadness. It was disheartening!

But yesterday, as I visited a young mother with heavy burdens—as I was on my home visits for the St. Vincent de Paul Society—she embraced me with a heartwarming smile. With a babe in arms and another child making mischief around the living room, she was "*transfigured*" by her smile, even though she faced many struggles and responsibilities. The example of Jesus' Transfiguration conquered disfigurement, even through a simple smile. Share your smile with someone and make their day! It did mine.

REFLECTION 5

The turn around

Something marvelous, *and dangerous,* happened to me the other day. Recently, I have been asking family and friends to write a brief reflection for a book I had been writing about *the Holy Rosary*. This is an excerpt of the first reflection I received:

> "Unless I take time to turn down the volume of this inner cacophony and (at least momentarily) actually silence this inner voice, I don't think I can effectively pray because I believe prayer is more about being open to *listening* to God's "still small voice" (1 Kings 19:12-13) than it is about *what I say* to God. I used to think of prayer as being a way to ask God to help solve a problem, whether it was a problem close to home or halfway around the globe. And, while I still think that is partly true, I've come to believe that the *way* God answers prayer is not by intervening into earthly affairs as a *separate* force. Rather, I believe God intervenes through any one of us who hears and follows God's promptings. That requires that we take time to *listen* to God's promptings expressed to us in a quiet voice that usually is inaudible and only heard in solitude…"
>
> Steve M.

Steve M.'s reflection was a life-changer for me. It spoke deeply to my practice of praying the rosary, and how, recently, praying it had become more of a burden than a blessing. I have gone through these phases before. I remember after praying the rosary every day for nine months (August 2008 – May 2009), I began to feel dissatisfied and even disillusioned with the rosary. It turned out to be not merely the repetition of the basic prayers, but the repetition of the Holy Mysteries (stories of Jesus' life). That's when I began to piece together the ideas of creating the extra 3 sets of 5 Mysteries—which eventually turned into my book, "Journey with the Expanded Rosary," that I finished writing in 2015. I was writing a sequel to the original book until the other day, when I read Steve M.'s reflection.

no accidents

Faith calls us to see that
  there are no accidents—just God-incidents
    tested by Rwanda and the Sudan
      with crippling violence and slaughter
        how could there be "no accidents"?
        I guess it occurs in how we deal with
        what happens to us

> one sage said, "it's not what happens to you
> it's what you do with what happens to you"
> and the God-incidents arise like the phoenix
> in the choices we make, the decisions
> we follow thru on that lead to growth,
> wholeness, health and a loving response

Corsair

Something has shifted inside me now. How do I begin this new journey of writing the sequel without stepping on my past writings, my stated beliefs and my former statements of allegiance to the power and beauty of the rosary and Mother Mary herself? I did not know.

There is one thing I do know to be true here, though: my personal spirituality does and always did reach far beyond my devotion to the rosary. No offense, Mother Mary—but, besides providing comfort and structure, the repetition of the *Hail Mary* and the *Our Father* seems to have often left me in a mundane, muffled déjà vu that enslaved my creative mind rather than freeing it.

"Unless I take time to turn down the volume of this inner cacophony," wrote Steve M., *"actually silence this inner voice, I don't think I can effectively pray* because I believe prayer is more about being open to listening to God's "still *small voice" than it is about what I say to God."*

Steve M.'s words hit me like a rock in the forehead! All of these hundreds of times I had prayed the rosary, WORDS filled my mind. Yes, the prayers often became informal mantras, allowing my mind to drift in reverie about the Mysteries, or about a related personalization of a Mystery (such as praying for those with severe back pain – while praying the Mystery of Jesus being scourged at the pillar).

Over the years, I have had myriad prayerful, blessed moments while praying the rosary. Yet, the rosary is words, words, words—no time for silent, reflective discernment. Have I been praying fervently with concise cognition as my main force of good? Where do I meet the SILENCE that Steve M. speaks of as so crucial to his prayer life?

Present

> when we're here
> THERE
> seems so tantalizing
> when we've got free time
> wasted time is so coveted
>
> absentee motivation seems to be the reality
> wanting to be there   when we're here
> lack of ability to live in the present
> always wishing for and never reeling in
> what we're hoping and pleading for

then not wanting what we got when we get it

so, we can say a little prayer:

*"God, please help me be who I am
how I am,
where I am,
when I am . . .
help me be truly present today!"*

Corsair

Listening to God—this is something that I never really thought about much while praying the rosary. Oh, I take that back. Often, while imaging a Mystery, I would be "listening" for the messages God wanted to give to me in my imaginative prayer. But *silent* it was not. It was almost always active with color and form and pictures of the life of Christ, or whatever related images I was imagining.

Although, I want to express that in all the times I have prayed the rosary—all the words, all the images—I can scarcely remember a time when I had a negative or destructive thought. Oh yes, I have lived through the horrors of Jesus' Passion on Fridays—with the Sorrowful Mysteries—dozens of times, but even then, my thoughts were in many ways "serene" because I knew the outcome of His death was the Resurrection!

It is such a mixed bag now that I have begun the process in THIS book to unravel the essence of my core spirituality. I want to believe in myself enough to see myself as worthy of sharing it with you—and worthy of being heard. Why would MY spiritual journey be of any relevance to you?

The answer to that question is only answerable by you, the reader, in as much as you find it interesting to grasp the ideas and images set before you here. But I can say this—I am just a fellow traveler on the journey we all take to find Truth and Life in our lives. And my story is authentic and real. This is my gift to you.

REFLECTION 6

ME, BIPOLAR?...A LOOK AT CRISIS '80

Yes, I have **bipolar**—bipolar disorder, which is "a chemical imbalance in the human brain that can cause dramatic mood fluctuations, behavioral disturbances and brain dysfunction." This is my personal, non-scientific, but hard-won, layman's definition of the illness.

We all have our ups and downs, ins and outs. It's just that, with bipolar, the chemical imbalance can make these shifts more pronounced, destabilizing and longer lasting. They are mood fluctuations that are caused by a combination of: situational stressors, chemical imbalances and the *awareness of the history* of both that have influenced habits of thought and behavior to create this disadvantaged state.

I have Bipolar I, the more severe type of illness with, generally, "higher highs, and lower lows." Bipolar II displays a phenomenon called "hypomania," a lower-stage mania with many of the same symptoms as full-blown mania—racing thoughts, heightened energy, euphoria, unrealistic self-esteem, over-spending, over-verbalizing, over-most-everything, etc.—but at a lower level. Although, even though I have Bipolar I, I have experienced hypomania recently, also.

I take numerous medications to keep my system stable—actually, "uppers, downers <u>and</u> in-betweeners" —that strive to give me a chemical balance to keep me functioning well. And, generally, they do! I am very grateful for my meds, because, without them, I am left in a very compromised mental, physical, spiritual and emotional state.

There are other factors that also keep me stable: social contacts (my wife, Sandra, family, friends, coworkers, parish members, social organizations and social occasions), spirituality/religion, physical fitness, proper diet, sleep (absolutely crucial), and interests and pastimes, etc. When I am at my best, I lead a fairly "normal" life. When bipolar is getting the best of me, I can be a real mess!

Below is a poem portraying a view of bipolar that may be helpful . . .

Bipolar...the tiger in my pocket

wouldn't you know
that the very pain and disillusionment I thought was long gone
rests wearily...anxiously...even comfortably...
in a beast-caging pocket
stitched into each garment of my life ~

be it physical, emotional, intellectual or spiritual ~
affecting every experience—day and night . . .

what is this creature, you wonder?
I have **bipolar** . . . *a tiger in my pocket!*

imagine an old car with a malfunctioning thermostat
hot and cold unregulated—off & on, & off . . .
from frozen and too cold to start,
to bubbling over, red-lining in heat

<u>this</u> is bipolar disorder—at the extreme edges

there is no ditchin' it, no stowing it away in a corner cedar chest
no chaining it down in dungeon dark

song goes,
"You can't take a lion and throw 'm in a cage
and expect 'm to be thankful for the shelter that you gave . . ."

this is the reality of the tiger in my pocket
it's NOT going anywhere so I better be aware of its motion
or, like a scorpion on the collar, it <u>will</u> sting
    (and it may just sting anyway,
        no matter how aware of it I think I am)

the illness has its abrasive, unpredictable side
at times like a "low-flying bomber"
dropping bombs of anger, criticism & judgment
on anyone in its flight path

at other times creating dungeon-thoughts
and dagger-emotions that keep me locked away
in pitiful silences of screaming ugliness

yet sometimes the tiger purrs with a gaze of brilliance,
    cuddly love & powerful, helpful words
        …magic-maker, genius creator……deceiver

greatest gift has been to have family and friends
who have hung in there with me
from lighthouse…to ocean buoy…to life-ring…to surf board

I happen to have the <u>best</u> crew swimming at my side!
they make life livable, fulfilling . . . and often enjoyable

> helping me to
>> *name,*
>>> *tame* &
>>>> *claim*
>>>>> the tiger in my pocket

    Corsair

In January of 1980, half way through my senior year in high school, devastating changes were to come. In the little rural hometown of Buffalo, near Minneapolis, Minnesota, I was the "lone nester" for a mom and dad who had raised 8 other kids in our house. Sibling-wise, I was "all alone" for the first time since gestation!

All alone? Yeah! I had followed my brothers and sisters all my life, acting the way they acted, eating the food that they ate—being "a Melcher" the best way I knew how. "And now, how do I be me?" How do I cope with not having my next older brother there for me to sheep aside his "shepherdliness"—gladly <u>and</u> resentfully, for me. I was gladly *alone* the fall of 1979, earlier in the school year—a jock—co-captain of the Buffalo High School football team, captain of the hockey team, and tuba player in the marching band! Plus I had the prettiest girl in the entire school for a girlfriend! I had it all!!

But on came the self-conscious, self-doubting and self-questioning moments, that January 1980 night, after going to the Buffalo High basketball game with my girlfriend. Having held her hand at the game, and recently telling her for the first time, "I love you"—the innocent interpersonal intensity accumulated as I sat in that Lay-Z-Boy in the family room after getting home from the game. I began thinking—and pondering: "Hey, I don't REALLY love her—and if I told her I loved her and I don't, how could I love my parents?—or my brothers and sisters?—or my friends?" My first *shame spiral* (a downward spiraling state of anxiety, self-pity and regret) had begun. And in 15 minutes of agonizing, downward thought, I was deep in a psychological trauma-state called *depression*.

I didn't sleep a wink that night, or for four days after! I was a train wreck, already happened! This was the very beginning of a landslide depression that lasted 4-5 months, quickly deteriorating into a state of suicidal thoughts and half-hearted attempts.

These events swirled into what I call *"Crisis '80."*

The worst part was that I had <u>no</u> <u>idea</u> I had bipolar—or even that bipolar <u>existed</u>! I was blaming myself for my emotional distress, the condition raining down shame and disgust—and burdening me with thoughts of self-destruction, for no real reason. I was psychologically stuck, chemically stuck and emotionally stuck! Although I was uninformed and misled, it was nobody's fault. Bipolar was not the well-known ailment that it is today. From Abraham Lincoln, to Carrie Fisher (of Star Wars fame), to Catherine Zeta-Jones to the late Robin Williams—bipolar is nearly a household word now! It was even called "manic depression" back in 1980, currently carrying the euphemism of "bipolar," a much less descriptive term. Kind of ironic, isn't it! You'd think, in time, it would become a <u>more</u> descriptive term!

Below are a few paragraphs from my journal that help describe my situation with Crisis '80, and, in time, subsequent revelations:

Bipolar Balancing Act 2009

> It was the loneliest place in the world—to be in the agony and confusion of bipolar depression and having <u>no idea</u> that bipolar depression even existed! Having been a happy-go-lucky high school senior, my acting skills were tested to the max as my depression pounced, and I had to fake that I was still the "me" I had been weeks before.
>
> Amazing how the gruesome feelings of putrid depression stick with you—like pine tar on a telephone pole, under the surface. The only way for me to break loose has been to put pen to paper and set my soul free from its prison of despair.
>
> Hundreds of times in past years, writing has come to my aid in the fearsome face of bipolar depression. Words have comforted, informed, enlivened, clarified. They have spoken truths that my mind would have never come to without the process of thinking, writing, reading—then writing again. It's as though a silent angel rested upon me the first time I began journaling, on March 31, 1982, not long after my initial depressive and subsequent manic episodes in 1980. I had no idea I was a writer. I guess I wasn't. But now I am—thanks to having a crucial topic to write about—my mental health, my bipolar experiences. Bipolar has brought me the gift of *expression*. It is not merely a scourge—it has also been my saving grace!

The depression, which had its short-term, relieving reversals, at times, lasted through graduation, in June, then into the summer. Three crucial factors brought me up to an uneasy state of equilibrium: I no longer had "THE EYES" of the Buffalo High students monitoring my every move; I had my old summer job back at my Dad's construction company; and I could see the fruits of my labor (even if it was just cutting pipes with a blow torch and stacking the pipes in a pile). In high school, I rarely SAW the fruits of my labor, except in art classes or athletic competition!

This shift of moods only lasted a month before they, unknowingly, started to escalate and, eventually, I was on a "manic rise," motoring towards full-blown mania! Again, I had NO IDEA what was happening to me—only that it felt fabulous to be active, full of life again, and interested in most everything! This was a welcomed change from the sluggish, morose, suicidal moods I had been in for so long.

As August 1980 came, I was highly manic, and went on a trip to Montana and South Dakota with 7 of my buddies from high school—in a huge van, close-quarters—rambling across the plains and up the mountains of the West. This proved to be a disaster for my relationships with them because, in my manic state, I was irrational, uncontrollable and unstoppable. At one point I called out to quickly stop the van so I could run out and take a picture of a bison that had just crossed our path!

Also, danger was no obstacle as I climbed out onto an ice ledge, just for kicks, which could have resulted in a fatal, 4,000 foot fall! Those were just a couple of the extremely abnormal and disturbing moments that led me to losing all 7 of my friendships, one by one. By the time we got back to Minnesota, my manic antics had left me with a gaping hole in my social sphere.

I soon entered college by joining the Mankato State (Minnesota) University football squad, three weeks before classes started. But I continued my unusual behaviors even as my mom came down, 80 miles, from our hometown of Buffalo, to see me in our first pre-season football game. To her dismay, I didn't even acknowledge that she was on crutches, having sprained her ankle that morning. Also, I showed her my dorm room where I had a cabinet full of sweet rolls and doughnuts that I had collected from the breakfast line, for future munching! She was appalled, and immediately "coaxed" (ordered) me to come back up to Minneapolis to get a "psychiatric evaluation."

In my manic state of deep denial, (I exclaimed, "This is not <u>MY</u> problem, it's <u>YOUR</u> problem!!"), I refused—then acquiesced because she and Dad said I would not be rejoining my teammates or going into college at all if I didn't submit to their request. They saw something as severely wrong—I didn't! But I got the eval, and I was uncomfortably diagnosed with "manic-depression," which infuriated me because of the descriptive pronouncement—MANIC –Depression!! Reluctantly, I began taking the little pink mood stabilizing pills anyway, that day, and every day after.

Within three weeks, I had come down from my manic castle and back into a somewhat-stable reality, "down with the common folk." It was only at that point that I saw that my rolling all over campus in bright blue tennis shoe roller skates, with big yellow wheels, was probably not the wisest thing and smarting off to 270-pound football teammates was not the smartest thing either.

THIS was my first encounter with bipolar disorder! Since then, I have had many ups and downs, sideways shifts and confounding crossroads—too many to mention at this time. But this first episode was the worst!!

It is now clear to me that bipolar has been **a blessin**g (as we will see later) **and a curse**, and always will be, in my life.

REFLECTION 7

Poor in spirit

*"Blessed are the poor in spirit,
for theirs is the Kingdom of Heaven…"*
(Matthew 5:3; the Beatitudes, Jesus Christ)

It was at Sunday Mass, at All Saints Catholic Church, (in Milwaukee, Wisconsin), in fall 2018, that I had an epiphany: I realized that <u>I was one of the "poor in spirit!"</u> The sermon, which centered on this verse, Matthew 5:3, "Blessed are the poor in spirit," pointed out to me that my faith life was deficient in many ways. Or that's what I thought, at the moment. I was deeply consoled that Jesus had a special place in His heart for the downtrodden, the broken, the faith-challenged. I was in good company! Also, I was encouraged by the realization that I don't have to have it all together, that my poverty of spirit could become my strength—'When I am weak, then I am strong'—(Apostle Paul).

Years earlier, I wrote:

the hole

there was a hole
in St. Francis of Assisi's garb
by his shoulder—egg-sized
in a picture on the cover of his biography
it suddenly occurred to me that THIS represented the
poverty of spirit I had been hearing about
a hole in the tattered clothing of a poor man

poverty of spirit
when you know—<u>you just know</u> you have a *lack*
when you can see that
a part of you will not be satisfied—maybe never
a brokenness, emptiness, possibly a crushed identity

but it is in this very hole that God may do the best work
because God knows the power of **_mercy_**

and its redeeming qualities
that can make a wayward soul come to life again

I have been there—have you?
in the hole of emotional distress
in the hole of psychological stress
in the hole of physical duress
pretty familiar territory for many—
intimately known by many more

yet there is a comfort and solace in being aware
of a personal poverty of spirit...
to be at peace in the midst of this lack
knowing that the light of Christ can shine
through any darkness, in any place, at any time

if you sense *a poverty of spirit* in your life today
rest in it knowing how
the freedom of a trapped miner
comes in discovery of a light-flooded hole above
. . . and you shall be set free too

Corsair

How can a hole in our lives HEAL us? One way is through the humility and surrender it takes to admit we <u>have</u> a hole in the first place. Recognizing our poverty of spirit, this seeming lack of faith, ironically, can increase our faith and healthy dependency on God for our protection and sustenance. We gain a "clean heart" as we purge ourselves from beliefs such as "I can do this on my own" or "God will never forgive me!" Such pride and guilt, respectively, can only deepen the hole and make it a place of disdain rather than a place of refuge.

Place of refuge?—a hole in the soul? Sure, a "poverty of spirit"-hole is a place of recognition, not a place of resignation. Is this hole meant to be filled, mended, by LOVE, which comes as a gift from God? This hole is a part of our authenticity, our true selves—maybe it's not meant to be filled—maybe it's a sky light!

What about the hole being a part of our authenticity? Vulnerability as an asset?

Yes--in fact, if we only center on our "authentic greatness," we may be overlooking a huge and valuable part of ourselves, because our beauty comes in our overall authenticity—the good and the not so good—<u>our complete selves</u>. For none of us is perfect, and it is in this imperfection and struggle that we may often see our most powerful attributes—strength, resiliency, patience, kindness, hope, brawn—gifts that may not be visible in authentic greatness.

St. Francis of Assisi did not try to reform or transfigure or get rid of his poverty of spirit—he embraced it. He accepted himself AS HE WAS! He saw himself as fully dependent on God for his sustenance and hope. In the words of the Gospel song, he saw God as "his all in all!"

Do I need to deny or eradicate my poverty of spirit in order to live a balanced, happy life? No, not at all! I can wear the garment, like St. Francis did, with a spiritual hole that displays my humanness and brokenness before God and still be OK.

*****an alternative viewpoint . . .

After some thought and prayer, I realize that I may have been speaking of giving in to mediocrity and scarcity. I am NOT a St. Francis and cannot live in a deficiency state for very long. If I don't even TRY to raise myself up, if the poverty of spirit keeps me from trying to be my best, it is not of God. Poverty of spirit means I am dependent on God for my SPIRTIUAL sustenance, and for my overall wellbeing. It is a state of BEING—being in connection with God.

I don't think Jesus wants us not to strive for *authentic greatness*. And, not being a saint, I think He wants me to get out of that hole-ridden cloak and into some comfortable clothes, not torn, not dirty, not drab. Jesus wants me to be a whole person, not a "*hole person.*" This means striving for my best and giving thanks for every positive step I make to better myself and the lives of those around me.

This "hole in my garment" can be replaced with a new shirt—one that gives me dignity and honor. But I still can remember the one with the hole in it. My *poverty of spirit* is not merely lack, but changing out the garment all together into a newer and fuller ME. I need not wallow in self-deprecation or pity, but overcome my deficiencies to live a fuller life, in Christ.

St. Francis may have been able to live a life of lack and deprivation, but I am not a saint. Jesus never said, "Blessed are the poor in spirit—and may they ever remain poor in spirit!" I believe he wants us to become more independent <u>and</u> to approach a more mature dependency on God. We are meant to soar, not to live in a hole, or give in to living there. We have the power to make positive changes in our lives—and I believe God would want us to make those changes.

"Our complete selves," (mentioned 7 paragraphs earlier) is not meant to glorify or promote "the bad" in ourselves; it is a higher calling to IMPOROVE these parts of ourselves—not to deny or hide our brokenness, but to move through and beyond it.

If we remain in a poverty of spirit mode, mediocrity or self-deprecation should not be an aim, but something to work our way out of. Replace the hole, the cancer, don't just fill it in or mend it OR leave it wide open! This, I believe, is God's call. Then we will be in a better place to serve others, and to fill the world with more beauty, not just duty.

REFLECTION 8

LAUGHTER

Humanity is infected by the virus of laughter. (Corsair)

Picking my oldest brother John up from the seminary one sultry summer afternoon, in 1971, or so, Mom decided to stop at Target to *"pick up a few things."* John, behind the wheel, refused, but finally acquiesced with Mom's insistence that "It'll only take a few minutes."

My brothers Jim and Charlie were deployed to get a box of flaked potatoes and some liquid laundry detergent, respectively, and I was sent off on a special mission to get "cinnamon panty hose," of which I had no idea what I was looking for. Jim came back to the counter with the flaked potatoes, Charlie with his detergent—munching on a long bag of free popcorn—and I was lost somewhere in the *spice aisle,* looking for the cinnamon panty hose. Good luck!

Finally, I gave up and sought the Melcher clan somewhere near the front of the store. I found them waiting in line behind a lady with a ton of items in her cart. (My brother John was waiting "patiently" in the car). We waited and waited. Mom gave up on the cinnamon hose (and so did I). We finally got to the counter, and the cashier was punching in the prices (like they used to do), each with a separate "code" to tell what kind of product it was. Mom had gathered 10 items, and we had them all sprawled out on the conveyor belt.

"Oh, we forgot the ketchup!" spouted Mom. Jim ran off as the items neared the end of the conveyor belt. Meanwhile the cashier, of which it was her first day, realized she had put in some of the wrong codes and was getting frustrated. Jim came with the ketchup, a couple of minutes after everything had been rung up. The cashier was beginning to quake.

She called for the manager, and the two of them worked on the codes. Then, the final straw. Mom looked in her purse—NO WALLET!! Mom stealth fully called out to her boys, "Head for the door!" as the cashier began to cry, leaving the whole mess behind!

When we got to our get-away car, John was beet red with steam blasting from the top of his head! He had kept the car running, thinking it would "only take a few minutes," and the station wagon had run out of gas!

Begrudgingly, John put the car in neutral and we tediously pushed it 150 yards, up a slight incline, to the Target gas station, quickly filled up and zoomed towards home! There was nothing to be said. And nothing was said.

This was the Melcher "TARGET story"! Do you have your own Target Story in your family?

REFLECTION 9

JESUS CURES THE LEPER

Mark 1:40-42
A leper came to Jesus (and kneeling down) begged him and said,
"If you wish, you can make me clean." Moved with pity, he stretched
out his hand, touched him, and said to him, "I do will it. Be made clean."
The leprosy left him immediately, and he was made clean.

But did you notice? The leper came to Jesus <u>knowing</u> that he could be healed. He knew Jesus could do it, if He wanted to. His belief, his faith, not only brought out the healing qualities of Jesus, but the healing qualities within himself—the *placebo effect*. Do you think he would have been healed if he would have gone up to Jesus with the attitude of "Well, I don't really believe in this healing stuff, but I guess I can take your word for it that maybe you can heal me"?

Not only would Jesus not have the motivation and energy to heal (although he could have either way), but the man would not be in the receiving mode; he may not have been able to hold onto a healing touch if he <u>had</u> received it.

As another example, Jesus spoke truth when He told the woman cured of hemorrhaging that "Your faith has healed you." She believed, she <u>knew</u>, and, indeed, she was healed!

Author Louise Hay, whose cancer was healed through the grace of persistent positive affirmations, said, "What you choose to think about yourself and about life becomes true for you." Somehow the leper knew this, and had faith that Jesus' compassion would reach out to him and bless his leprosy away. You see, his belief made it possible—Jesus' grace made it happen!

REFLECTION 10

Jesus Found Safe in the Temple

Three reflections about *Jesus Found Safe in the Temple*

A. It's hard to fathom the depth of relief Mary and Joseph must have felt when they found Jesus in the temple. The lost-ness displaced by the shock of a blessing—the boy found after 3 days of searching everywhere. They probably were going to the temple to offer sacrifices to God in hopes of being blessed with their son's "<u>found</u>ation."

Being found is one of the most beautiful experiences in the world—not only for the person found, but for the finder. Jesus seemed to be surprised that His parents wouldn't know where He had been hanging out. He was surprised at their surprise! His parents probably experienced the relief-followed-by-anger response---"Oh, thank God you are safe, but how could you do this to us!?" Then a heavy, long hug. Being found is a strange and wonderful experience!

B. Mary and Joseph have some responsibility in this too. They assumed that Jesus was with relatives in the caravan that headed back to Nazareth. They weren't <u>sure</u> of where he was and they didn't bother to look. So when He came up missing, some of their emotions must have been guilt and remorse that they had not been better stewards of their son's welfare. So when they discovered Him in the temple, part of their relief must have been out of their own mistake at assuming they knew where He had been. Jesus wasn't the only "guilty" one.

C. Who was really lost? Jesus or Mary and Joseph? Yes, Jesus had been lost by them. He could not be found. But He was in His Father's house—the temple. While His mom and dad were the lost ones. They were lost in fear and grief and guilt and worry. So, Jesus was not the only one found safe in the temple.

Have you ever felt lost? Have you ever "lost yourself"? It is a horrible place to be. I can relate to the scene of Jesus being lost. Can you? What is your experience? And if you feel lost right now, can you ask to be found in the heart of Jesus, our Savior?

REFLECTION 11

CALLED ME BY NAME

Have you ever been called a name? Instantly, you probably thought of a bad name, a teasing name. But what about a good name—possibly a nickname that suits you, or a name that may add a bit of levity? Can you think of a name you have been called—a name you like, or possibly cherish? Names are very significant.

Isaiah proclaimed, **"The Lord called me from birth, from my mother's womb, he gave me my name."** Isaiah spoke with authority, in Isaiah 49:1, about his mission and purpose—to help Salvation reach the ends of the earth. He seemed to realize that, as his mission was to spread God's Word, it was also to know himself and the reason he was born. Isaiah was a major prophet not just because he had the most chapters in the Bible—66—but because he spoke from the depth of his being, from his authentic self, allowing himself to be a vessel to transmit God's holy messages.

Doesn't this sound a lot like someone else in the Bible? Right. Jesus. How often was Jesus known to say that His purpose was to spread the Good News or to shepherd the flock? He had a distinctive name—Emmanuel—which means "God with us"—that describes well His true being—a name which rightly identifies Him.

Jesus has numerous names: Redeemer, Prince of Peace, Defender, Mighty Counselor, Good Shepherd–all which describe aspects of his Presence in our lives. The one that actually describes the Trinity is "LORD." We have all heard of "Lord God, Almighty Father" and "Lord Jesus Christ"—but remember this too; the Holy Spirit gains this title also, in the Nicene Creed: "I believe in the Holy Spirit, the Lord, the giver of life." The power that names have is remarkable!

In the Gospel, the story of how John the Baptist received his name is chronicled. Eight days after the baby's birth, Elizabeth, his mother, proclaimed that his name would <u>not</u> be Zechariah—as it was customary for naming a boy after his father—but that he would be called John. Then they asked the boy's father, whose voice had previously been silenced, and Zechariah wrote, "John is his name." Was this a coincidence, or a calling? Time proved it to be a calling.

The old saying goes "What's in a name?"—and this is a very good question. We all probably want our names to be known for sincerity and love; remember also that "God has called YOU by name" to become more authentic. What name do you take in as your own, and how does it identify you? As a Christian? As a child of God? As a loving human being?

gentle spirit

gentle spirit
        come to me~
                gentle spirit
                        help me see~

        of all the multitudes
          you chose me
        you've called me by name
                  gentle spirit
         come to me

            Corsair

Reflection 12

Charisms

The flame is fanned by the gifts God has given you. (Corsair)

What is one excellent way to discover your God-given talents and abilities?

Charism. Have you ever heard that term before? My wife, Sandra, and I have been involved with a program entitled "the Called and Gifted Workshop," where participants are encouraged to take a 120 question inventory to begin determining their giftedness. Such areas as "leadership, service, writing, teaching, faith, knowledge and giving" are included in the group of 24 *potential* charisms.

What makes charisms special is that you can discover new and exciting aspects of yourself that can assist in becoming *your* best self. As Elizabeth Gilbert, author of <u>Eat, Pray, Love</u> said, "You don't receive gifts coming FROM you, but THROUGH you." Actually, of the 24 potential charisms, only a few will be discerned as true charisms, because the definition of a charism is **a truly extraordinary gift one is given from God, at Baptism or Confirmation.**

    much more than

        recently read   *we are all much more than we seem*
        wise words that rang clear in my heart and soul
        as if hearing a brand new song I've heard all my life
        it is great that there is
        someone out there who sees Life similar to my vision
        that we are all gifted to be designers of our destiny
        and coached by a Creator who brings cosmic significance

        these words spoke truths that we are
        much more than
        we have ever imagined ourselves to be

        it is in the simple—often trivial—glance at our inner-selves
        that we discover the magic of our existence, our passion—
        and what would have happened if we didn't
        listen to the glance at the mysterious
        or hear the scent of the unspoken textures

> that often go unnoticed in the dust of daily living?
> they'd be found lost in our own unknowingness
>
> being and knowing *we **are** much more*—
> this is where we belong
> in the mix of passionate observance
> fighting distant brokenness
> and hearing callings we cannot yet decipher,
> but feel, none the less
>
> **here we are**—who knows why—but in this <u>here</u> lies
> the fact that the depth of our world's heart
>   yearns to cry out
>
> ***"We are <u>all</u> much more than we seem!"***
>
>   Corsair

In the inventory each potential charism has 5 questions, and one is asked to rank each question a 0-3 scale, "0" being "never," "1" being "little," "2" being "some" and "3" being "often." It is brought out that a "0" is a good answer because the inventory is searching for your true opinions, and "never" is an honest assessment. Interestingly just because someone has a 14 or 15 (highest rankings) on an item in the inventory, does not mean they have a charism.

The "3 F"s describe what is required for a true charism:

- F1 = **Feeling**—how does it feel when you are involved in the action? Are you moved spiritually, as if it were a form of prayer? Do you feel good—are you "in the zone" when doing it?

- F2 = **Fruits**—what are the positive outcomes of your doing the activity? Are you blessing others with your actions? Is it doing what it is meant to do?

- F3 = **Feedback**—what kind of feedback are you getting about your potential charism? Is it encouraging?

For me, I had a 15/15 on my inventory for WRITING. I have great **feelings** when I am writing meaningful and spiritually-focused and/or self-improvement material. The **Fruits** are evident in the books, poetry and articles I have written, and I have received very good personal **feedback** from numerous people about my writings. It is evident that I have a charism in writing.

One does not have to have a high score on the inventory to have a charism. For instance, "faith, wisdom and knowledge," three in the inventory list, did not receive very high scores on my inventory (9, 9 and 5, respectively), but are all involved in my writing charism, and their affiliation may mean I have charisms in one or more of these areas. I do not know yet—I need to go through a discernment process before I know.

to be

    prove
        move to
            improve

never again trying to be something
    for someone else
        but only trying to be

to be

        my best self

    Corsair

"Discernment" is the process of figuring out, through experimenting with it, if you do indeed have a charism—if it is not an obvious one, like my writing charism. It means using the potential charism in real life and looking how the 3F's are playing out.

This whole process is very exciting to me and I am planning on getting more involved in teaching, coaching and administrating the inventories and other various aspects of the program. I believe discovering your charisms is a blessed opportunity to find out more about yourself and your gifts—so you can give them to others around you.

Trans form a tion

we have got a choice
a very simple choice
do we want to live a life of   imitation   and   envy
or a life of
        possibility and opportunity?

choice that will either launch us into new heights
of risk and struggle—hope and adventure
or dig a trench of complacency and anti-compassion
encouraging a raw negativity that can squander great gifts
and crush creative endeavors?

this may be the most important choice of this week
    month   year   or your life
to find freedom from fascist fruition of fateful fancies

CHOOSE LIFE

choose life

      is the call
    of the wandering heart
can't you hear it?
it's *possibility* and *opportunity* that cry out
to us when we seem to be falling
into the rut of blind imitation
and ugly envy

what choice will <u>you</u> make
today?

Corsair

REFLECTION 13
Humility

It was a conversation with a friend that brought me to a new place. We were walking on a quiet city street, sunny afternoon, when I began to share with her what I considered a personal blasphemy. She was intrigued and asked me to go on. I considered her a highly spiritual, traditional Catholic young woman—maybe not the right person to share this personal admission with, but I took the risk and went on.

"I really don't believe Jesus suffered as much as I have." She listened intently. "I have suffered for over 28 years with bipolar disorder—the strain, the loneliness, the hospitalizations, the depressions and manic bouts—if you count all that up, it adds up to be much more than 24 hours of excruciating pain of His Passion. At least Jesus only had to suffer for one day. I've had all those years! He hasn't gone through what I've gone through!" And with a light touch as if a butterfly were landing on my shoulder, she said, "He did."

I stopped in my tracks, on the pavement and looked at her in amazement. "What you went through, *He was there*—He went through it <u>with</u> you." I was shocked—not that I didn't believe her—but at what I knew to be true. Jesus had carried that cross for me to Calvary <u>and</u> all the way through to that moment. It was one of the most humbling, ego-deflating moments of my life. Suddenly I had realized that I was not alone—never alone—in my struggles! And Jesus still helps me bear my cross today. His example of tenacity and perseverance challenges me to trudge through my daily struggles and confront the major ones. It's amazing what a little conversation with a friend can do. It changed a whole world view, my way of thinking, my whole heart-position, and brought me back to a spiritual reality that encourages hope and resiliency. This friend wanted to see growth in me, and make it stick. And it did.

on the way to the cross

when the bully dug a trench for me to bury my dignity alive
You filled it with Your Love, oh Lord, and helped me to survive
~ it happened on the way to the cross ~

then the teaser spoke words of hurt and
untruths about my character and You came upon the scene
to displace the slanted detractor
~ all on the way to the cross ~

RICH MELCHER

a push and shove came my way to disturb my peace
and you steadied my mind and cooled my temper 'til anger ceased
~coming to me on the way to the cross ~

when crushing anxieties filled my heart and mind with pain
You gave me a glimpse of You at the rock
where you knelt that fateful night, once again
~ blessing me on the way to the cross ~

and when I rise above troubles and Your Resurrection
I clearly see, I know You knew this was Your ultimate destiny
~ as You toiled on the way to the cross ~

so how do I meet my daily trials and pains?
I recognize You on every step of the way
rising above with joy as I say,
"I found You on the way through my cross!"

Corsair

REFLECTION 14

Peaceful Prayer in the deserted places

In Mark 6:31, Jesus describes "retreat" perfectly: "Come away by yourselves to a deserted place and rest for a while." I can imagine what He was wanting—rest and relaxation, time for self-reflection and replenishing of spiritual batteries, renewal of a sense of hope and resilience. Jesus probably wanted this and even more for the disciples.

Who knew that the crowds He had been ministering to had another version of "come away"? They would follow this man wherever He went. They would be so "on Him" that Jesus and His apostles couldn't even enjoy a quiet meal together. The crowds would be like *the paparazzi of the poor*, drenching Jesus with needs, needs, needs.

Jesus took it in stride because He had pity on them, seeing them as if they were "sheep without a shepherd," and He gave away His retreat to serve them. The Gospel doesn't mention how the Apostles felt about such an intrusion, but I can imagine they were quite distraught. Could they keep up with this man's zeal and strength?

How do we deal with disappointment—such as a loss of time for us to rest and relax? Well, we have a Savior, Jesus, who showed us one virtuous example of personal sacrifice. Do we have the courage and stamina to do the same?

In the Scripture one Sunday, Jesus tells his disciples, *"Come away by yourselves to a deserted place and rest a while."*

As He often sought quiet, deserted places to pray, Jesus meets us in our deserted places. Often Jesus was dealing with people who were lost—in some way or another—lost in hunger (mental/physical/spiritual), lost in sin, lost in darkness, lost in immobility, lost in pride, lost in destructive ways. So, too, Jesus meets us there—in our "lostness." And He wants to help us find a home.

When have you felt this "lostness" and sought a deserted place to be with our Lord? Isn't it amazing how aloneness can bring us to a place of contemplation and deeper faith, if we let it? I hope YOU can find these deserted places in your life so you can break away from the pressures of life and experience Jesus' deep touch into your longing heart!

the canvas of my heart

be my canvas, oh spirit of Truth
 to guide me ever on my way
  there to enlighten and to soothe
   my journey throughout the day

a canvas of Hope, a canvas of Peace
 You guide me at every turn
  my pain and sorrow to release
   old memories no longer to burn

be my canvas, oh Lord, in every way
 readying a place for paint to rest
  in a multi-colored majesty
   as I give the world my best

letting go of outcomes and selfish desires
 You bless me with a fresh place to paint
  Your canvas, clean & white, inspires
   the blessings fit for a saint

be my canvas, oh spirit of Love
 to guide this shepherded path
  send me gracious blessings from above
   and bless my weathered shepherd's staff

help me mold this staff into a brush
 to paint Your Will in colors wild & free
  so as to adorn Your canvas in a silent hush
   as I become the painter You want me to be

        Corsair

REFLECTION 15

INTEGRITY BUBBLING UP

Exploring a few moments of despair and hope . . .

                               p
                       u
      integrity   bubbling

        funny how a guy can go for years and years   *believing*
one thing (or, at least, believin' he's believin')

       & suddenly   past images surface
disappointments, disillusionment, disagreement,
         discouragement, disregard
              all come

      bubbling up

      day turns into night (a fright, at first)
     then the silent stars and yearning moon
    come clear visible in the grand darkness
  having patiently waited in blinding day-stream
as if a forlorn lover gazing steadily across long waters
        in direction of distant mate

    this missing love
  this shipwrecked seaman
      has cast his net upon me
       and <u>he</u>
        is
       ME

his long-buried treasure—gold coins flung at my feet
  is the realization of true inner longings,
    once-blanketed observations

and a sturdy hull of indomitable integrity
this ME
has reclaimed the fertile soil of my unkempt
but dazzling soul
not as if a flag planted stiff on dusty lunar surface
but oak roots strong and wide-reaching
anchoring trunk transformed into an ever-widening,
multicolored upward spiral
no longer a prisoner of benign yet besieging
false fantasy friends
that for so long kept the blinders and earplugs secure
no more   no more
lie uprooted & Truth revealed

Corsair

REFLECTION 16

A Fool on Fire

When confronted with the extremes of bipolar disorder, I experience **the height of my despair and the depth of my JOY!** It is a paradoxical, strange, exasperating, wondrous, ugly, confusing, exhausting, beautiful world. The cost is my sanity, my awareness of self, my security.

Bipolar has been a vague friend of mine for over 39 years. I say "vague" because I have not had it as bad off as many other people I know who have a mental illness. I used to give talks on bipolar, partnered with others who had mental health diagnoses. The accounts of their experiences with mental illness often made my story sound like a cake walk. Sure I have had my "ups and downs," but not the trauma and substance abuse and violence and homelessness that many others have experienced.

No, I have never been homeless or lost all of my teeth or been shot or even broken a bone. So what is so compelling about MY story? Well, we all do have our own personal drama. I present you with my mental health story…

A Fool On Fire

beats a genius on ice

by Rich Melcher, December 22, 2015

Ah, Paris!!—spring 1980. At seventeen-years-old, and a high school senior, I saw the sights: the majestic Eiffel Tower, the magnificent Notre Dame Cathedral, the magical art gallery—The Louvre, and the mysterious Mona Lisa! But, in ugly irony, I also saw a Paris subway car coming down the tracks toward me and had thoughts of jumping in front of it.

What emotional **misery** could have caused such contrast?

And what a paradoxical flip-flop, only four months later when I became **a fool on fire,** excited about life, hyperactive and talkative beyond measure. I shifted from no self-esteem to explosive self-esteem; from blind in the dark to blinded by the brilliant light; from nearly hopeless to totally limitless—all in such a short period of time! THIS is a glimpse of bipolar disorder—"**bipolar.**"

Bipolar is a chemical imbalance in the human brain that can cause dramatic mood fluctuations, brain dysfunction and behavioral disturbances. Bipolar has had an enormous impact on my life (good and not so good) and with the help of professionals, family, friends, proper medications and God, I have been led on an eventful journey—one that I want to continue with you now.

I survived the dreadful depression that had me on that platform of doom in the Paris subway, in the spring of 1980. Yet, in just a short amount of time, I became over-active, over-disclosing, over-everything!!—blasting through that first manic episode in late summer of 1980—just as I was launched into college.

I developed a voracious appetite and talked, at length, with nearly everyone I met—probably making more enemies than friends. The funny thing is that I was living out a perfect metaphor: Having purchased a pair of bright blue tennis shoe roller skates with big yellow wheels, I was literally "on roller skates," rolling gleefully around the campus of my new college.

Imagine the looks I got! And imagine what was going on inside my mind! Distorted? Unrealistic? Delusional? You bet! I knew no boundaries in my elation. I was a free spirit, unaware of the chains bipolar had on my psyche, locking me into a prison of childlike speech and behavior.

Luckily, my mom witnessed these and other bizarre behaviors and lured me into getting a psychiatric evaluation, just before classes started. Help arrived in the form of a little pink mood-stabilizing pill, and within a few weeks, I had leveled off—for the time being. My first depressive and manic episodes—something I never dreamed could ever happen again, was under my belt! And I had survived!

deliverance

Oh God, please release me
from the dreadful slavery of my past
I pray You let me see the good
in the now and let peaceful moments last

it's an emotional quandary to suffer
from deeds of days gone by
and only see the negative, the mistakes
& the regret in a shadowy mind's eye

I pray for deliverance, oh Lord
please part this inner Red Sea
and let Pharaoh-thought of past defeats
sink and drown in front of me

I thank You now for this work
You're creating deep inside
no more to run, no more to slip and fall
nor shamefully to duck & hide

Corsair

Thirty-five years later, having had many dramatic ups & downs, ins & outs and overs & unders, I am—by the grace of God—still here to tell you about my challenges with bipolar. And I am grateful for this opportunity to share!

Before we go on, I want to know if you realize the risks I am taking by sharing these details of my life with you. Do you see how I risk alienation?—how I risk having your opinion of me forever altered because of my personal disclosure?—how I risk no longer being taken seriously, or worse, not even being heard?—how I risk being seen as different—strange—weak? Mental illness stigma is real! So why would anyone risk self-exposure on such personal mental health details? And why does it matter?

Because if my story can bore even a peep hole through the thick, rock wall of mental illness stigma so someone can see the view from the other side, I will have been successful.

Bipolar has been my ambiguous companion all these years. At times leading me into dreadful and even dangerous states of depression, then launching me into the soaring, ebullient heights of mania. Yet, often bipolar has left me resting calmly—in complaisant camaraderie—in the stillness, deep within. Bipolar has always been present—waiting, hovering, lurking.

desperate

words to describe my un-in-it-ness

I DON'T CARE
   screams in my head
     high above
the city

screaming in vain

  nobody hears
    nobody is meant to hear

     cry hallow   but full
    into the nothingness

      no answer

Corsair

My first depression doused me with anxiety and corrosive insecurity in early 1980, during my senior year in high school, as I mentioned earlier. The worst part was that I had been shackled by the belief that whatever was happening to me was all my fault; that I somehow brought it upon myself. If I only knew then what I know now—that I had a "serious and persistent mental illness," then-known as manic-depression (now called bipolar disorder), I would have probably avoided much of the pain and suffering. This <u>not</u> <u>knowing</u> lasted far beyond the time when I experienced my first depressive and manic bouts in 1980, and eventual diagnosis.

Actually, the <u>not</u> <u>knowing</u> lasted until 1986 when another explosive manic episode landed me in a hospital for the first time in Milwaukee, Wisconsin. Surprisingly, in those six years, no one ever sat me down and explained the complications of living with bipolar. Also, for those six years, somehow, my hometown pharmacist was mailing me a usually-prescribed substance—a psychotropic medication—with no clear directions and using no prescription! <u>And</u> I never once saw a psychiatrist! For 6 years!! It was outrageous!! But I had no clue! I just thought I had "<u>a</u> <u>condition</u>"! I received no words about a mental illness and took the pills out of blind obedience and habit, not out of consciously seeking treatment, stability or recovery. In fact, I never heard the term "RECOVERY," probably well into the 1990s. It is common term in mental health and substance abuse lexicon now.

I vividly remember a crucial moment after I had had that manic overload and subsequent breakdown in February 1986. It was right about the time when the Space Shuttle Challenger exploded and went down in flames! After my breakdown (which ironically matched the image of the Challenger's demise), I looked out from the hospital room window in Milwaukee, across the cityscape, and spotted the high school at which I had been teaching just a few days earlier. It suddenly struck me that I would never go back there again as a teacher. I thought, "I must be crazy! My career is over!" At age 23, I felt banned, stigmatized, branded.

But a psych tech (a worker only at the level of a nurse's aide) at the hospital felt my desperation and reassured me that, indeed, I was NOT crazy, and that, in time, I would be able to lead a healthy, productive life again. "Rich," he said, "you are a person with a mental illness—NOT a mentally ill person!" There have never been more reassuring words in my life—not from <u>any</u> doctor, not from a priest, a nurse, a teacher, a parent, or even a good friend! Such encouraging words came from that insightful psych tech. Wisdom can come from the most unlikely places!

song

and the song says

we are the prisoners
of the prisoners we have taken

so often this is true
we go for so long with
NO FEAR
then suddenly find ourselves
10, 12, 20 years back
in seemingly the same position
situation
as that far-back person

> "How could this happen?
> Haven't I out-grown this?"
>
> security and poise are *temporarily* shaken
> but we realize it was just a glitch
> and even from this, too, we can learn
> (isn't that the point?)
>
> so it's good that we see
> we need to let go of the controls
> and let God fly the plane
> as we head calmly, reassured
> to stable distant destinations
>
> Corsair

Most people don't know the simple facts that one out of five Americans has a mental health issue, and one out of 25 will experience a serious mental illness, such as bipolar, schizophrenia or major depression in their lifetime! *But remember,* ***I am a person first****—a person with a mental illness, not a mentally ill person.* The psych tech in Milwaukee made that clear to me, way back in 1986. You see, I have been mentally ill—sick with the illness of bipolar—but I am not ill right now. I am NOT mentally ill! I am striving to be balanced in body, mind and spirit. Still, if I lose touch of any of these three, indeed, I could become mentally ill again.

I remember a time when stress and a medication change threw me completely off balance. It was 1999 and, during a delusional manic high—on a whim—I flew from Des Moines to Denver, and then on to Salt Lake City in search of a job with Dr. Stephen R. Covey—author of the best seller, The Seven Habits of Highly Effective People. In my deluded state, I just knew Dr. Covey would hire me on the spot, after he heard how I revered his work and followed his program.

Hours after landing in Utah, I vaguely remember standing, exhausted and disoriented, in a hotel lobby and the next thing I knew I was being handcuffed and stuffed into a police car. Then I blacked out. Somehow, the next day, I was on a jet headed back home to Minnesota, still dazed and unaware of what had happened.

slanted self

in the presence of my
        s
         l
          a
           n
            t
             e
              d

self
i see the true me
in spite of the tolerance inside
i view ugly *what-has-not-been-done*
and all the idle potential

i can feel
myself slipping into
a calm hatred
of all this that has been wasted
in my presence
in my custody
all the consuming—and little giving back
this throbbing abscess tooth just waiting to implode
and smash my self-image into shards of fun-house mirror

never to see my true image again
dangling
destiny can be a killer
all the wait on my shoulders

all the wait

Corsair

I believe that psychotic mania, as it is called, causes a state where the unconscious mind overrides the conscious mind's decision-making processes. The unconscious mind takes over, as if living out a dream. Interesting that my unconscious mind, in this manic state, focused on a personal development guru, Dr. Stephen R. Covey—and how I dreamed of working for him, being willing to do <u>anything</u> (such as flying half way across the country) to make it happen! But, here's a scary thought: What if my mind had been filled with visions of hurting others, of anger and retribution—where would I have ended up? Killing someone? In jail? Dead? Anything could have happened—but it didn't—thank God!

I have never been able to figure out exactly why some manic episodes are "happy" and some are "intense and potentially destructive." Maybe it has to do with stress, or sleep changes, or stage of life? Why do I become manic—or depressed, or a mix of both? I know when I'm heading for the downer of depression if I begin to have low moods, lack of interest in <u>everything</u>, low energy and if I start sleeping too much. But, the high side, proceeded by what I call a "manic rise," is much more difficult to detect. It hides itself in the energy and vibrancy of the moment. Even though depression is obvious, mania is dripping with denial and sneakiness.

It occurs to me that, in a sense, bipolar plays games with one's self-esteem. In depression, I was lost—little-to-no self-esteem detected.

hurricane

and so
once again
the hurricane hit the beach
(never dreamed I'd see another)
after all those I've lived thru

forecast had been sunny
vision clear and thoughts riding free
and yet the trade winds of my mind began to swirl
and high waves, choking my heart, came crashing in
on the beach of my soul—my personhood

lost

once again
but this time with a better shelter
than past perfect storms

do I fight against the raving
or ride it out sheltered?
(knowing that storms "don't last always")
I can feel the heat—the heat of depression!

don't run away
face your demons

but do I face them by trying to change
or understand
or let them be?

I really don't know

Corsair

With an elated form of mania, self-esteem became inflated and magnified. In fall of 1980, when I was manic for the first time, I had ridiculous dreams of becoming a professional football player, a Minnesota Viking! Hey! Doing 10 pushups would have been a stretch!

Unrealistic? A cornerstone for bipolar mania! I felt TOO GOOD, with too high an opinion of myself. While, in depression a few months earlier, I felt horrible and had an awful opinion of myself. These fluctuations of mood *wreaked havoc on my emotional, psychological, intellectual, social, physical and **spiritual** being.* As you can see, self-esteem is deeply affected by the ravages of an out of control bipolar event—either manic or depressive.

After all the bad places I have been with bipolar, I have always been able to be resilient—to bounce back—and, God willing, find my way home again. Living with bipolar has had a lot of ups and downs. I've had to start my life over a number of times. Luckily, I haven't had to start from zero and work my way up—but, let's say, from 50%. This meant such things as reconstructing employment, mending important relationships and regaining self-esteem, to name a few.

My life has been stable for seven years, (this reflection was written in 2015) which has brought me to a good place where I am working in the mental health field as a certified peer specialist, and I am a cast member in *Pieces*—a mental health advocacy play produced by NAMI (National Alliance on Mental Illness). Also, I share my bipolar story of hope and recovery through NAMI's *In Our Own Voice* program. Yes, I realize, that's a lot of mental health activities! But, you know what they say—*"grow where you're planted!"* So I've set down some roots!

Like I said, for the past seven years I have been stable . . . but what happened seven years ago, you might ask?—my most mysterious and troublesome relapse ever. Just before marrying my wife, Sandra, in October 2007, my psychiatrist became alarmed by **the possibility** that my kidneys were being damaged by the mood stabilizing medication *I had been taking for nearly 30 years—the "little pink pills."* He pulled me off it completely, abruptly—cold turkey! Within a week, my mental health had been compromised and I was confused, disillusioned and angry. Angry is hardly the word for it—how about *infuriated*!

anger fills

what is it when anger fills
my very soul
as if water in a bucket
to be dumped off a bridge

anger fills
this heart of mine
and has scatters my conscience
like seeds to the wind

anger fills
the Presence of my Lord
which is washed out
in a hatred spun so deep

anger fills
me with a disgust for
all
all that is good and
all that is bad

anger fills
my unspent time
and broken windows
of a lost hope

anger fills
my unique and ultimately
different self
in so many ways
it's hard to count

it's painful to be different
when *the same* is relished
and the unique is odd and ugly

I find ways
to hate myself like nobody's business
and it is nobody's business
so there

Corsair

Although the wedding went very well…the medication mix-up was the doorway to an unstable 2008, mainly due to the fact that I was experiencing what I now see as "dual personalities." In some ways, this has actually been a reoccurring phenomenon in my life since my first manic bout back in 1980.

But it was magnified during my manic state in 2008, which brought in this confusing dual-personality factor. I would shift, with no warning, in and out of "me-now" (pointing to my chest) and a greedy, back-stabbing, manipulative personality that I call "SHAM".

From February to October of 2008, my personality would shift from SHAM to the "normal me," like the easing in and out of a clutch on a manual transmission. Using a computer analogy, these shifts were not merely like changing *documents*, but more like moving between entirely different *operating systems*. There were actually two personalities—Rich and SHAM!

It was as if SHAM had taken over the pilot's seat in the airplane of my conscious mind. He had bound and gagged me, and stuffed me behind the seat—facing forward. I could still see and hear all that was going on, but SHAM had the controls.

The odd thing is that I was totally unaware of this at the moment. Only in reflection after the crisis had passed did I discover the eerie dynamics of my SHAM personality. That's when I decided to give him the name "SHAM"—which means *to falsely present something as the truth.* That fit well!

The consequences of SHAM's influence were devastating. They ranged from employment instability, to unrealistic educational aspirations, to extreme interpersonal difficulties — especially with my wife, Sandra, who had to deal with a man who left her five times in 4 months. The final move involved storming away from our comfortable 3-level condo in Milwaukee to a small, second floor apartment in Michigan. Talk about a downgrade—not only in living accommodations but in relationship investment!

I wasn't aware of it at the time, but I left for that last time on September 15, 2008—the exact date of the massive American stock market upheaval and ensuing recession. But in my extreme self-centeredness—or, should I say—in SHAM's self-centeredness, I was lost in an inner world where all areas of my life were falling to pieces—and I didn't even know it! Surprisingly, I was absolutely unaware of the goings-on of the outside world.

aware

it seems like every moment goes by
like the flash of a bird's wing
thoughts filling in spaces
like some intellectual hour glass
grain by grain the pebbles of the moment
land on one another and shove
down
   down

life is a vast unawareness
a broken watch spinning freely
in its own reality toward
unknown destinations and transitions

what I wouldn't give to be aware
to live in THIS moment
to be free of the baggage of unawareness
that so often fogs my memory and distorts
the present—like some huge smudge on a windshield

Corsair

Three weeks later—by the grace of God—on October 6, 2008, (ironically, the date of Sandra and my first wedding anniversary), I fell to my knees in my Michigan apartment, in a sleep-deprived breakdown. Due to lack of sleep, my manic mind had begun short circuiting and decompensating. I was struck down by a sudden, staggering thought: **"I think I really have a problem!!!"** This blessing in disguise was a shocking revelation, and within one minute, in an amazing moment of liberation, I broke through the soap bubble of delusion and denial that had kept me trapped in the slanted world of my alter-ego, SHAM.

I quickly got up off my knees and called the hospital, and within an hour, I was on my way to get help. The denial had been shattered and the delusions evaporated! This was one unique occasion when mental health decompensation actually worked <u>for</u> me, to help break down the denial system that had captivated my psychological and emotional life for months. With one more milligram of my anti-psychotic medication, a good night's sleep and a call in to my wife, Sandra, to begin mending bridges, SHAM vanished and has not shown his face since!

When "the real me" surfaced from the disabling grip of SHAM, and I returned to our home in Milwaukee, Sandra and I had to regain our footing as a loving married couple. Mainly, Sandra had to regain her trust in me. Once I had identified SHAM as the instigator in the unfortunate consequences of the relapse, as I crafted a book on the happenings, the momentum of forgiveness and reconciliation brought us back into experiencing a healthy, loving relationship, once again. She had eyes for me again—and I for her! Long Live Love!!

eyes

we lock eyes
I share with you
the ME
I'm unable
to see
or maybe
the ME
I have trouble
showing to myself
or even the ME
full of passion &
playfulness
or could it be
the ME
searching for
significance
acceptance
connectedness?
but then
you free
inside
the joy
and wonder
as you
give my selves
back to
me

Corsair

Clearly, I had made mistakes, yet I had choices. The **real me** was still acting within the SHAM personality. I–me now—made mistakes. Sure, at times, we make mistakes; but you are not a mistake, nor are you the struggle itself. Guilt means "I made a mistake;" shame means I AM A MISTAKE!" This was not a shame-situation.

As a result of experiencing trillions of thoughts and feelings over the past 50 plus years, I have received the gift of a positive, energetic power within me—which some call intuition. I call it *Corsair*. Named after a World War Two fighter plane that fought over the South Pacific—*my favorite airplane*—the Corsair has a 2,000 horse power engine and sleek gull-shaped wings that make it a unique, powerful flying machine—an empowering image of how I see myself!

My Corsair airplane, (which has been modified, in my mind, to have no guns, bullets or bombs), is a symbol that represents a vibrant, protective, freeing force within me. The powerful, liberating influence of the Corsair image drew me so close in early 2008 that I legally changed my middle name to "Corsair." Like a *still, small voice* within, Corsair (which is my personalization of *the Holy Spirit*) was there later in 2008 to protect me, even when hope ran thin because of the SHAM intrusions. There was Corsair, often gently whispering over my right shoulder—words to calm, words to inform, words to bring peace. Corsair has helped me rise above some pretty tough situations, such as the treacherous encounters with SHAM.

Now that I have given this stabilizing and comforting phenomenon a name (Corsair), looking back, Corsair has been my emotional, intellectual and spiritual companion, during the best of times and the worst of times. From encouraging me to see the beauty of the Rosebud Indian Reservation, where I visited my brother John in 1982, to cautioning me when a college professor in Construction

Management challenged me with his worrisome, unethical advice that same year. His shady actions caused me to reevaluate and switch my major to Mass Communications—writing—a much better fit for me! Also in '82, Corsair put my pen to paper as I began writing my journal, on March 31st, which has produced thousands of pages of journal entries, scrap booking and poetry—and, in time, seven books! (I guess 1982 was a pretty BIG year for me!)

I know it must sound like I have all these voices rolling around inside my head. Actually, I do not "HEAR" them. They are not audio hallucinations—they are merely thoughts and feelings that often compete for space on the surface of my conscious mind—that *still, small voice*.

SHAM, the devious one, (the separate personality, the alter-ego), had distinct deceitful inner-workings that caused so much trouble.

creeping out

everything is poem
when mania creeps out
of its damp, dark, mold-covered cave
so delighted to see its own reflection
in pen & purpose

purple passion

leaks out of old wineskins
of depression and captivity

yet poem is not as important as poet
the words in volley are mere
expressions of self
not self
itself

manic trains of thought with no apparent track
wind among the smoky hills of a deeper mind
sometimes leaving engineer behind
in dust and gravel

hope lies in bending of rails
to bring the wild iron horse
back home again
to rest in the station of peace
awaiting freight of less weight
and passengers of promise

Corsair

But, deep down—somehow—he was a part of me, loitering in my unconscious mind. I believe SHAM is a part of what Carl Jung called "the shadow." While Corsair offers healthy spiritual guidance and encouragement, sometimes SHAM's "voice" was louder than Corsair's, especially when he tried to slam me to the mat in 2008. Corsair and SHAM portray the age-old struggle between the competing forces of good and evil. Gratefully, Corsair prevailed, and his presence has played a huge, positive role in my success.

As you might have guessed, I have had more manic bipolar incidents than depressive ones. Yet, at times, when I get bogged down in feelings of self-dissatisfaction and lack of accomplishment, I can become vulnerable to what I call a "shame spiral." A shame spiral is an emotional implosion where fear of the future, current displeasures and past painful events suddenly appear, like a submarine splashing to the surface. This puts me in a tailspin, hurling me downward into distress, regret and remorse—my mind eventually spinning into what I call a "mini depression."

A few years ago, while caught in a shame spiral, I wisely decided to envision myself in the cockpit of my beautiful, imaginary orange Corsair airplane. In my imagination, I firmly pulled back on the stick and the plane came out of the deadly tailspin just before hitting the ocean. Then, in my mind, I pulled the stick back even more and cranked the throttle, and with the 2,000 horse power engine roaring, my Corsair airplane slowly began to rise. Simultaneously, my mood was rising right along with it! Up, up, breaking through the clouds and into the sunshine. Amazingly, my mood and attitudes mimicked the visualization! No, I didn't suddenly feel bright and cheery, but, in just a couple of minutes of creative visualization, my mood had been elevated; hope had been restored, and I was thinking much more positively.

This Corsair visioning pulled me out of a dangerous shame spiral. I learned that night about the power of imagination to influence my psychological and emotional wellbeing. Creative visualization, in the form of my Corsair, became a driving force in my recovery.

The idea that "It could never happen to me again" became a defense mechanism over the years. It buffered me from paralyzing anxiety and fear after numerous bipolar episodes. But now I realize that I am not out of the woods, nor will I ever be invulnerable to emotional or motivational setbacks. It is sobering to know that, like taking medications for the rest of my life, I will always have to monitor triggers—like stress and confusion—to remain aware of my bipolar tendencies. Yet, I think it is better to be more realistic and not pretend that my difficult experiences have made me immune to any and all bipolar influences.

At some point in life, one needs to take a good look around and define what success means to them. -Thelma Golden, a major influence in the art world, needed to see her differences not as a disadvantage, but as an advantage. She needed to show her REAL self and to define her success on her own terms.

I have chosen to see my bipolar as an advantage, evident in the many mental health activities I have been involved in. My experience is valuable, especially as a certified peer specialist, where my lived-experience is shared with mental health clients to promote recovery. It's a true blessing that one of the main job "qualifications" for being a certified peer specialist <u>is that you have a mental illness</u>. Wow! How times have changed! How many jobs have this as a requirement for employment?

Lou Tice, co-founder of Pacific Institutes, speaks of taking set-backs as temporary and that winning is built on positive expectancy—this is success!

Gaining from mistakes has been a theme in my life for over 20 years. But, success is much more than just gaining from mistakes, although that is important. For me, success with bipolar is living a balanced life—body, mind and spirit—and being able to express myself in all areas of my life.

dream come true

how can I know when my dream comes true
if I don't have a specific, enduring dream?

does the leaf fallen from toppled tree
canoeing dangerously down meandering stream
know where it is going?
only knows that it **IS** going
for a fantastic ride
on this river of life
no rudder
no keel
no map
no wheel
but going
all the same

Corsair

Creativity, compassion and optimism are three gifts bipolar has handed me. And, as "CREATIVITY" is one of these **bipolar gifts**—I have had to do a lot of re-creating! Starting over is a difficult process, but a necessary step if one is to regroup and move on. The great thing is that one gets to decide which direction to go in *recovery*. And, hopefully, that's in a better direction than before. Sometimes the only way to go is up!

There *is* hope in recovery! There is ALWAYS hope! But no one has to go it alone. If you or anyone you know is suffering from a mental illness, reach out! Get help! I remember what my mom firmly told me when I was deeply depressed in 1980:

"I can see that you are suffering. You are not alone. This, too, shall pass."

Very wise, very helpful and very true. You never know how a kind word or gesture may bring someone back from the edge.

One day, as I struggled in my spring of my Crisis '80 depression, trying to hide my pain and anguish from my classmates in high school, I found an envelope taped to my locker. In it was a card from Margaret K., a person I hardly knew. From what I remember, the greeting card read something like:

**"I can see you are having a hard time lately. Keep the faith.
I believe in you! You will find your way!**

Your friend, Margaret."

A special angel at that moment, Margaret will never know how—at least for that day—she helped me step back from the ledge of my suicidal ideations and experience a little yellow blossom of hope. She reached out as a friend, and, somehow, it led to another day, and another—one little blossom after another—until the depression had lifted.

When souls meet

God

Dances

Corsair

If there is one thing I have learned in my life, it is that we may never know what emotional state someone is in until they tell us, or if we ask. Who knows—they might just be having the worst day of their life; they may have a house in foreclosure, a dying loved one, a broken relationship glaring in their face, or a mental illness that is bearing down on them. You may be catching them at their very worst moment! So, my advice? Be kind and understanding! You will often never know how you affect others, so you need to be the best example you can be, as often as you can! Someone else's happiness, or even their life, may depend on it.

Everyone has got a mental health story. Some may not be as dramatic as mine, some much MORE eventful—but we all have our challenges—**We've All Got Something!!**

I've heard the saying, *but for the grace of God go I….No matter how bad you think you've got it, there's always someone who's got it worse.*

I've had it BEST today, since I have had the opportunity to share with you about the uppers, downers and in-betweens of living with bipolar. I have truly enjoyed sharing it and hope you have too!

Thanks!!

Rich Melcher

REFLECTION 17

Paying patience

Lack of patience is one of the greatest downfalls of society today, in my view. Just the other day someone honked at me for stopping while clearing the intersection in front of him, when my left turn yellow arrow had turned to red. I had been halted by the car in front of me turning left and was merely following him out of the intersection. What's the point of honking? Intimidation? Sharing simmering annoyance? It worked—it did annoy me!

When we look around this world, we see rampant impatience, from the grocery store aisle, to the pressure put on news media to get a story out quickly without having all the facts. It's as if we're gerbils spinning the wheel but not getting anywhere. Maybe we all need a bit of mindfulness.

Who am I to talk about mindfulness, one who struggles with it every day? But here goes.

I believe we seem to lack a sense of mindfulness—that practice of fully, nonjudgmentally experiencing that which is in and around us. The dictionary describes it as *"a mental state achieved by focusing one's awareness on the present moment, while calmly acknowledging and accepting one's feelings, thoughts, and bodily sensations."*

Jesus displayed this mindfulness---"awareness on the present moment," exhibited often in how He interacted with those around Him and with His Father. In your imagination, picture Jesus when, perhaps, He could have thought . . .

faith being forged

faith
    hot iron tested
      orange glowing
        pounded out
          by My Spiritual Blacksmith
            Father God

My questions
  My doubts
    My will to truly understand

and fully believe
valued
in a process so personal
so substantial
so simple as
prayer

from quiet longing
to silent acceptance
Father God respects My process
of slowly being transformed from
boiling molten iron
to long red-hot bands of steel
then to useable, approachable, palatable products
only created through the furnace-driven ways of

faith being forged

Corsair

This takes patience—to live faithfully in the present moment—to appreciate what is around and inside us. Jesus had this mindfulness, this sense of *"peaceful patience."* Jesus knew, coming into Jerusalem, that "this was it" for Him. He had predicted and pronounced His death many times to the Apostles, although none of them "got it," (or wanted to *get it*). How could He travel on down that road into the city of His doom with such confidence and conviction? Wouldn't He have shaken that donkey right off its feet as He lumbered into Jerusalem, palms being spread on the streets?

But He didn't tremble. He had a **peaceful patience**, even in that time of enormous stress. His biggest fear seemed to be that the citizens of Jerusalem would try to make Him king—earthly king—something He was dead-set against and had avoided many times before. But the palms in the road, the "Hosannas" (which meant, among other things, "come and be our king to drive out the oppressors"), and the cries of joy all added up to exuberance—and trouble.

It was such a paradox that, at the pinnacle of His "career," His ministry, He would be brought down so quickly, and condemned to death, in just one week. Yet, His peacefulness prevailed, even into the moment of the Last Supper when He knew He was sharing His last meal with His friends. Jesus exuded courage, stamina and a "cool head" in the face of His ensuing Passion. He is THE example to us all that one can "keep the faith" even in the face of the most challenging times. He had many moments of **peaceful patience**!

REFLECTION 18

Say "Yes!!!"

Can you say YES to God? Actually, this poses a very puzzling question: What would you be saying YES to? In the Gospel choir in which my wife, Sandra, and I sing—at All Saints Catholic Church, (a Black Catholic church in the heart of urban Milwaukee, Wisconsin), we sing a song simply called "YES." The soloist sings over and over "Yes...Yessssss"—and at one choir rehearsal a while back, I began to wonder: do people know what they are saying Yes to? Do the members of this choir know and feel and live out this word? Are they doing so right now? Am I? And is it a question or a proclamation?

I have fought tooth and nail with this idea of saying yes to God. Many times I have given up on what I thought was God's will for me because of confusion, exhaustion or simply fearing that I might be asked to do more than I can handle—or am willing to do. And is there such a thing as YES if you believe in predestination?—the belief that all of life has already been planned for us, and we are merely living it out. No options. Just "truth."

I used to have a hard time with this until the day, back in 1994, when I first saw the movie *Forrest Gump*. Remember that movie? Tom Hanks played a cognitively-challenged man who was always in the right place at the right time—with the right insight and the right *heart*. It was a very meaningful and memorable movie.

One scene from the movie that has stuck with me all these years was when he was reflecting on his life and his many amazing experiences, like meeting four presidents, becoming a football star, a war hero, a ping pong champion, and a father. He also recalled many losses, such as losing the love of his life, Jenny. He expressed the most poignant and memorable spiritual comment that I have ever heard; let me see if I can paraphrase it:

> *Is it destiny or just out there free-floating on a breeze...*
> *maybe...but I think it's possibly both happening*
> *simultaneously...*

It was this idea that gave me permission to put to rest this battle raging within me between luck and predestination, and the feeling that I was not doing God's will every time I thought I failed. I also no longer had to depend on luck and superstition as my vehicle to discover meaning in my life.

When you understand yourself, when you have a hunk of self-love and a modicum of self-insight, it's much easier to say YES to what you perceive to be God's call in your life.

Take Mother Mary, Jesus' mother, when she was approached by the angel Gabriel who "told her" she was going to bear a child, the Son of God. She could have said no, or "not right now!" She had free will. She could have said, "No, that is going to be too hard, too stressful, too costly." She could have tried to whisk Gabriel away as a false prophet, just trying to trip her up.

But no—Mary trusted the angel's decree, and, I believe, the very moment she said **yes**, Jesus was begun within her womb. It may have been "destined;" it may have been God's will; but she still had to consent to this call of God. In joy, Mary instantly responded affirmatively. I believe, Mary's YES became the most important **YES** in human history, for God was allowed to work with and in and through her to create Jesus Christ—the Savior of the world!

Going back to our Gospel choir's song "YES," we say yes in so many different ways. We say yes to freedom, to inclusion, to feeding the hungry, to studying to make the grade, to laughing when it's time to laugh and crying when it's time to cry. But one of the greatest gifts is the freedom to make up our minds if a Yes is the right Yes for us, at a certain time and a certain place.

A friend of mine, Sue, had to make a faith-filled choice between a good career as a social program administrator and fostering her great niece who had been abandoned by many of the important people in her young life. The youth was having severe problems—socially and academically. Sue banked on the grace of God to help her make the right decision. She was giving up sure security for a life on Social Security to take care of her great niece, who had serious behavioral problems in school and a seemingly impossible time making and keeping friends.

But Sue made the daring plunge to come to the aid of the downward spiraling girl and, two years later, Sue is having the time of her life watching this 9-year-old turn completely around, under her guidance. The grand niece's grades are way up, and she is making friends more easily! Sue's prayerful and tactful YES has paid dividends beyond her wildest dreams!

I believe that God understands our hearts and is ready and willing to guide us into new realities, if we only let go and trust. The right YES will come.

REFLECTION 19

SAVED BY CORSAIR

"Confidence"…its etymology includes **with faith…to have faith in.** Confidence, belief and trust are crucial words represented by the word Faith; there's that word "confidence" again. How do we have confidence in ourselves?

For me, this has been an uphill battle. I don't blame it on my bipolar disorder, but it sure has played a part in it. My specialty? "Shame spirals": that's when vulnerability and self-pity gang up on me and send me reeling, nearly out of control, into my dissatisfaction with self. It's like, every negative event or thought or action that has ever happened to me surfaces, like a breaching whale, emerging from the top of the sea. The fury and clamor of the emotions cloud my rational mind, and I begin to spin downward.

Confidence, right? I want to dive into an incident I mentioned in Chapter 16 a little deeper. When I was caught in a shame spiral, thinking the very worst of myself and my situation, it hit me that I had an ally I hadn't called on before. It was my Corsair airplane. I imagined myself piloting my metallic orange Corsair, spinning down toward the sea, and grabbing the control stick hard, pulling the plane out of the death spiral—around 200 feet above the water's surface.

Then I cranked the throttle and pulled back on the stick gently, and the plane slowly began to rise. *Meanwhile, my moods began to rise with the plane—instantly.* In my mind's eye, the plane climbed up and up until it reached the puffy white clouds above. I leveled it off and soared ahead. *Moods stabilizing.* Then I cranked the throttle again and flew up into the clouds and right through them, into the sunshine and blue skies above. Finally, I eased back on the throttle to resume a comfortable cruising speed. *In three minutes, this visualization popped me out of my shame spiral. I was not feeling totally "normal," but no longer was I in that emotional downward spiral, and was ready to move on with my life, in a good mood and with rectified attitudes.*

Confidence—"with faith"—in self! But it does not always work that way. The other night, I began to go into a shame spiral and did NOT call on my Corsair to pull me out of the spin. I "positive-ized" my way out, bringing back, with the help of my wife, Sandra, recent good happenings and feelings that drew me back from the edge of despair quickly.

You may wonder, "Why don't you just call on God to help calm your thoughts?" In a sense, I am, by utilizing my imagination and intrapersonal resources to assist in bringing myself solace and peace. God works through my Corsair and my wife to bring imaginative and practical solutions to my emotional predicaments. God IS present and working in my life, at these times.

A SIMPLE PRAYER

GENTLE PEACE – SURROUND ME
INNER TURMOIL – RELEASE ME
HOPEFUL MIND – RENEW ME
GRACEFUL SPIRIT – FORGIVE ME
GAPING HOLE – FILL ME
SHOT-DOWN EGO – PROTECT ME
LOVING GOD – BELIEVE IN ME

Corsair

With confidence, possessing faith in myself, I discover God's plan for me. I may not always be aware of what direction to head, but, with God as my compass, I do get there. Bipolar has been a blessing and a curse. Sometimes giving me insights into life, energy, creativity and empathy for others. And at other times, it knocks me off my horse of progress. But, having confidence that God is always there with me and in me to help me figure things out—this gives me hope that I am never alone in this life and that I <u>do</u> have faith, even when I don't see it in myself.

REFLECTION 20
THE RROCKSS CODE

*"Don't worry about who your audience is
or whether it's worthy! Just write!"*
(Sandra Melcher support)

For the past 10 years, I have been working on an ethics code—a way to channel energies and direct my life. Actually, I have been thinking just as much about how to help others direct their lives, also. I've been writing about a way to entice others in seeking the value of observing a healthy, personal ethics code. Below is version #75, or so, expanded and developed, which I present to you in hope that you can gain a modicum of encouragement and a dose of strength and energy. My aim is for it to be a positive influence in your life. I call it the RROCKSS CODE.

the RROCKSS CODE
by Rich Melcher

R = Respect
Respect 1. I continually show sincere respect, for others and myself, by being patient, *nonjudging*, understanding and kind.

R = Responsibility
Integrity 2. I humbly acknowledge and gain from my mistakes—recognizing that *it is only a mistake if you learn nothing from it!*

O = Observation
Attentiveness 3. I gladly listen to others with focused attention and *provide genuine interest* in them and their various interests & perspectives.

C = Cooperation
Optimism 4. I courageously *seek the opportunity* in every difficulty, rather than spotting the difficulty in every opportunity.

K = Knowledge

Authenticity 5. I creatively discover, encourage and express my *authentic greatness*, while inspiring others to do the same.

S = Safety

Awareness 6. I significantly enhance integrity by forming and honoring healthy personal & professional boundaries.

S = Service

Gratitude 7. I thoughtfully express gratitude for goodness received <u>and</u> for undesirables removed or avoided.

Below is *the RROCKSS CODE* expanded and explained . . .

Respect is the foundation of all relationships, institutions and organizations—and our inner-selves. "*I continually show sincere respect, for others and myself, by being patient, nonjudging, understanding and kind.*"

Respect means trust, dignity and honoring of all. It is so basic that we often don't think about it. It just is! Sad thing is that *Respect* has taken a back seat in many ways in human society. From all the wars, hatred and discrimination, to the destruction of natural resources and the warming of the climate. Respect has all but been forgotten in many sectors of our world.

Especially with human conflicts…war, poverty and disease—to name a few—show how we have forgotten—or never learned—the meaning of RESPECT and the motivating and moderating force it can be.

Our Catholic Mass celebrant recently spoke of the Latin verb "*respicere,*" which stands for "respect," and how it means "to look again at"…yes! We think we know what it's all about, we make a judgment, we cling to it—then we choose **to look again at it** AND WE COME UP WITH A COMPASSIONATE, EMPATHETIC VIEWPOINT. *In a perfect world, w*e see ourselves in the other. We don't just go forward (or backward) with our first impression, but we seek out the good—we "F.O.G."—Focus On the Good. There we can find an optimistic situation or kind person beneath the veneer.

I remember speaking with an African American young man in 2005 who was explaining the terms of my apartment lease agreement in great detail. He was stone-faced and to-the-point about every section of the document.

Then, an amazing thing happened. Somehow we got on the topic of *12-Step groups,* and how we both had experience with them. Suddenly a welcoming smile arose from the ashes of his frigid face. Incredibly, I witnessed a complete transformation of this young man, to the point that I actually began to think I was sitting across from a different person!

He had a captivating smile which lit up his face like a bonfire. He had transfigured right in front of my eyes! And his voice became warm and inviting, also. Our respect for one another peaked as we shared our experiences and the mediocre engagement turned out to be quite inspiring!

A similar set of encounters happened when dating my wife, Sandra, as we expressed our love for one another:

when we said it

*tonight I told you you are special
and how much you mean to me
and I meant it…when I said it*

*we were in each others' arms
speaking our meaning to each other
and we heard it . . .when we said it*

*an unconditional love arose like the sun
or the moon—it breached the horizon
of our open hearts, as I spoke my love
and my word was true…when I said it*

a love like I've never experienced before

and possible plans for a future together
hearing the word of hope…when we said it

I thank God for you, you thank God for me
we have found something special in each other
budding soulmates in motion
in touch & deed & word…when we said it

Love, Rich

We MUST gain back the attitude of mutual respect if we are to solve the world's problems! Or the strife will go on and on. It starts with self-respect, then branches out from there. *A people without self-respect is a people lost.* We must be found in the dignity of RESPECT!

Responsibility flies the flag of "Integrity"…**"I humbly acknowledge and gain from my mistakes— recognizing that it is only a mistake if you learn nothing from it!"** This is one of my favorite ideas because it offers something we often seem to have so little of these days—**HOPE!**

We can take any moment of our lives, ponder it, think about how we may have committed an error, seek to rectify the situation in our heads and hearts, and do just that by formulating a new solution and replacing it with the old mistake. THIS is learning from our mistakes—(GFM = Gaining From Mistakes)—no matter how long ago; years, or just 5 minutes ago! THIS offers HOPE, to me—and hopefully to you! WE CAN CHANGE OUR WORLDS by re-imagining them and holding fast to the new version—the <u>now</u> *vision*! We become **responsible** for this new version and encouraged by its superior outcomes.

When we seek to find a new version of ourselves and visualize the changes, noting the alterations and tweakings, we change all of Creation, in our own simple and little way—or our spectacular and grand way!

For a long 28 years, I complained to numerous people about how, on my 2nd day of work—age 16, first job, just out of high school—at my dad's construction company back in 1978, I was persecuted by my boss about a stupid forklift. Razor (not his real name) called me into the warehouse and told me to "take that forklift and put that pallet into the corner!" I felt a twinge of anxiety run down my spine, but I dutifully acquiesced.

First, I didn't know how to run the forklift. Sure I knew how to use a manual/clutch transmission, but that was about it! And second, I didn't know what the heck a "pallet" was! So, with my best "fake it 'til ya make it"-attitude, I jumped on the forklift and turned the ignition. A red light came on, but no motor. Razor yelled out, "Push the button, you idiot!" (I was getting annoyed!) There was a black, rubber button there, and, sure enough, it started the motor when I pushed it. I put it in gear and, with clutch ½ engaged, it would not move. "Release the brake, you bozo!" he yelled. (Now, I was getting rattled!) I noticed this lever by my right side and slammed it down. Razor glared at me. (I was getting angry and embarrassed!)

Now I was rolling. I finally figured out that a pallet must be that 9-inch high wooden crate just ahead of me, and I fumbled with the hand levers to lift and lower the forks. Jerkily, I slid the forks into the pallet, lifted it, cranked the gears into reverse and backed the pallet away from the wall. As I lurched forward to "put the pallet in the corner," I could hear my boss spouting out screeching expletives as I finished up the job! (I felt humiliated and vulnerable—but victorious!).

> "Failure is, in a sense, the highway to success,
> inasmuch as every discovery of what is false
> leads us to seek earnestly after what is true."
>
> John Keats

For 28 years I had muttered out to people my sob/humorous story, until one day, it hit me! I had options! I had been so prideful about faking that I knew how to run the forklift—or could figure it out on the run—that I did not see how I had any responsibility in the escapade.

I did not have to be the victim! All I had to do was be aware and humble enough to simply say, "Mr. Razor, I have no idea how to run this forklift! Would you show me how?" And he would have had to teach me! (I would have felt humbled—possibly embarrassed—but empowered!) He couldn't deny someone's simply not knowing. He would have been obliged to give me pointers. But I did not ask him. I faked it, causing this whole drama to play out to its fullest, (I felt regret).

After those 28 years of anger and resentment, ONCE I REVISITED the dramatic images in a few moments of relaxed, creative visualization, and changed the responses and outcomes in my mind, I never again saw that moment of "forklift hell" as destructive or even embarrassing! (I felt revitalized!) It had become a massive learning tool for me. And it has no power over me anymore! **I truly gained from my mistakes!** I began asking more questions, admitting my lack of knowledge and observing my surroundings, (I felt, and feel, enhanced and grateful!).

This GFM, gaining from mistakes, is the essence of INTEGRITY, for me. When I found, within myself, the key to transformative change that lessened the burdens and maximized the benefits—then I was able to take full *responsibility* for myself and my life.

Observation implies that when we listen, we care. **"I gladly listen to others with focused attention and provide genuine interest in them and their various interests & perspectives."** They say that listening—truly listening—is one of the most difficult things one can do. To let go of your own agenda, your swirling inner thoughts, and focus completely on the other. This is multi-challenging!

In some cases, how do we show interest in something we are not interested in? Valuing. By valuing the person who is speaking and tuning into the topic of conversation—valuing the relationship, even if it is a brand new one or an old and deep one.

This is where the ugly phenomenon of bullying stems from—not hearing. Not hearing or caring to hear where someone else is coming from—only judging and persecuting, based on the appearance or behavior or "weakness" of the other. This stance comes from hate—hatred of self that filters down onto the world at large. Bullying is based on <u>de</u>valuing, on not hearing. It comes from "listening" to the prejudice and hateful thoughts that arise from ignorance and discrimination, compounded by peer pressure.

But when you really listens—body, mind and spirit—you pick up on the subtle nonverbal cues that provide relationship-building nuances, and the tenor of inflection that supplies a note of compassion and care that could otherwise go unnoticed. Reflecting a summary of that which is said back to a person shows that you are listening deeply and care enough to make sure you are getting a complete understanding. <u>This</u> is good listening.

I've learned that prayer is not merely stating a litany of requests to God but to listen to what God is saying to me. Much of my prayer has come in the form of writing and exploring the WORDS that appear on paper or on the screen. Through meditating on and imagining moments in Jesus' life, and by writing about feelings, ideas and observations of my impressions of "the Holy"—I have heard the voice of God steering me in one way or another. Upon more reflection of these transformative moments, I have heard the call of God, which is reflected in many of my writings.

right

in this pain, I write
in this darkness, I write
(yet, somehow, in so many ways
I'm attracted to the darkness)
in this room, I write
in this precarious state of mind

I write

in my search for God

I write

where—who—what would I be
if I couldn't write?

this scribbled raw clarity inside

blind desert lost

cramped trampled thoughts and emotions
breathe free on paper

right?

Corsair

By writing—I listen to my heart, mind and soul! Listening, in whatever form it takes, is the KEY to good communication, and it is a skill that can be honed with practice. When you begin by *providing genuine interest* and showing that you care enough to put some energy into it, who knows, you may discover that you are a better listener (or writer) than you thought!

Cooperation means taking on the challenge that "**we courageously <u>seek the opportunity in every difficulty</u>, rather than spotting the difficulty in every opportunity!**"

To SEEK THE OPPURTUNITY IN EVERY DIFFICUTY!!...<u>THIS</u> is one of the biggest challenges that we can face in life!! How many times have we complained about a person or a situation we were facing, with <u>no</u> intention or commitment to seeing the bright side or even acknowledge that we may be even a little off in our perspective or evaluation?

The word that gets me is "EVERY"...<u>every</u> difficulty. Now, it does not say that we are to make monumental strides but simply to <u>SEEK</u> THE OPPORTUNITY—to find <u>something good in every situation</u>. There still may be a lot of the problem remaining, but any progress is better than none!

(Below is a poem that describes my experiences in a Milwaukee
middle school, where I was left, on my own
—a teacher's aide—to "teach" a class of 5th graders
—for the whole day, more than once—although I had
no experience or teaching license, simply
because the school had a shortage of substitute teachers.
I had suddenly became that "substitute teacher").

deer in the headlights

saw the look in a child's eyes the other day
fear, dismay, confusion

deer in the headlights

(have you ever seen a deer standing stunned in the middle of
the road—staring at your headlights—as if in a trance?)

and it was probably the look my eyes a few days later
at school, where I was stationed
to do duties beyond my capabilities
(to take over an entire classroom, for an entire day,
with no training, no lesson plan, as a "professional" teacher—
yet only with special-ed. paraprofessional experience)
and left there in tension, fear & in a second-guessing mode

I bet I looked like a deer in the headlights too
stymied and stunted by my lack of knowledge & experience
feelings of shame, embarrassment, anxiety,

discomfort, hopelessness, tunnel vision,
& even self-deprecation that overcame me
like a cold, wet, salty wave splashing over my body
on a dreaded seashore

suddenly my old definition of optimism appeared
on my inner view screen . . . **"Optimism means
seeking the opportunity in every difficulty . . ."**
during lunch break, and I realized what my *opportunity* was
to **give** first-hand empathy and compassion
to the kids I'm tutoring (and teaching!) in that urban middle school

since I've been through it, just today, I find myself
uniquely qualified to recognize **the look,** and work
toward elevating the feelings of discomfort and disillusionment—
in my students and myself
I made the best of it!

it would be a lost opportunity
and a shame to leave this lesson only
in the space between my ears
and maybe I can help just one student
dodge the headlights of an oncoming inner-disaster
and find ways of relaxing and catching on to new ideas presented

(could THIS be a definition of joy?)

(((if only I experienced this courage and resilience every day!))

Corsair

This maxim of <u>seeking the opportunity</u> challenges me to fully look at my responsibility in the situation and see how I can alter it to make it better. It takes courage and determination—and energy and effort, plus a great amount of humility—to admit that I play a part in the inner-workings of the situation. It also means that I need to have a commitment to follow through on whatever findings I may uncover in the process of SEEKING.

It's so easy to "spot the difficulty." But to see that this is also a "missing an opportunity" position, it can become a place of loss and regret, if it is only focusing on the negative. We all can spot *the difficulty* — this is pure human nature. We notice disadvantages, recognize that our feelings get hurt; we see deficiencies—but then, what do we do with them? This is when seeking the opportunity comes into play.

Thomas Edison "sought the opportunity" every time he "failed" at another attempt to create the incandescent lightbulb. He explained it, after 10,000 tries: "I have not failed 10,000 times to create the lightbulb—I have found 10,000 ways NOT to do it!" With an attitude like that, how could he lose? He invented that lightbulb!

Recognize the negative impulses, pause for a moment and frame a positive response. Then, act out of this renewed framework to be at your best, even in a situation that is frustrating or even frightening or baffling.

Peacefulness

It was a time
When it was all laid out
Being the youngest of 9
Some call it childhood
I call it my own
Little piece of hell

Then came a time for a choice to be made
Choose fear and confusion
Or settledness and relaxed fit
And a choice was made—
(a little of both)

Comes a time in every life
To look back & view a self-gone-by
And choose whatchya wanna be
Now

In the stillness of a heart gone blank
Restlessness and trepidation arise
To create such a clamor and conflict
Of will <u>& passion</u>
That the choice must be made again for real

What to say to the inner-self
When this moment arises?
"Do I come or do I go?
Do I compare myself to a vagrant other?"

It's time
Time to choose
And I say "success fits you well
If only you grasp it like a glove and hold on"

Go on
Grab it

Know it
See and feel it
You are the one
The only one who can do it
And you <u>can</u> do it!

Now walk with me
Into your future
Alive
Free

Corsair

The opportunity to succeed and find fulfillment will appear when you focus on the positive side of the situation and avoid always spotting the difficulty.

Do you want to take the risk and supply the energy to be an opportunity seeker?

Knowledge of self is the key component as "**I creatively discover, encourage and express my *authentic greatness*, while inspiring others to do the same.**" Socrates exclaimed "The unexamined life is not worth living," and I high-five him on that! For 37 years I have kept a journal that has reached over 16,000 pages, to date. I consider March 31, 1982, the day I first put pen to paper, as my "born again" moment. This is where ALL of my writings originate. That everyday scribing of feelings and thoughts, or tapping on my computer—images and conversations—along with occasional scrapbooking—make me who I am today.

We discover our authentic greatness when we take an account of who we really are and acknowledge the gifts and strivings that make us special. We can see our God-given gifts and learn to express them in every way we can—through relationships, art, sport, profession, service, self-care, child-rearing, etc.

As mentioned earlier, another name for these God-given gifts is "CHARISMS." A charism is a special gift that we give to others and is inspired by God. The Catholic Church has a program entitled "the Called and Gifted Workshop" that provides a gifts inventory using 120 questions to "rate" 24 potential charisms. The workshop brings out our preferences and skills so that we can look at what we like to do and what we are really good at. Then, in a process of discernment, we come to see if it is just a skill <u>or</u> an extraordinary gift from God, recognized by our **Feelings** about them, the **Fruits** of the potential charisms and the **Feedback** that we get about using them. These *3-F's* help us see whether they are merely skills or charisms from God.

> (the first charism I am discerning is that of "writing"—and I am looking at poetry as a part of that gift...)

poet

what is it to be
poet
breeze flowing thru fingers
weeks and years of thoughts and feelings
found dancing descriptively
in lines of black & white
where distilled emotion
and focused images
find home

poet

be poet
be who you truly are
far from scenes of
comparison and affirming glances
here—finding self
on the pages of the heart

poet

recognizing a soul's breath
catching a butterfly then letting it fly free
       exposed for all to see
yet only liberated thru catching the wind

poet

finds the simple
and creates the important
where a mere observation
becomes an entire landscape
here life comes alive
and fledgling artist
becomes

poet

    Corsair

"Knowledge of self" means knowing our "authentic badness" too…the side of us that is not so pretty. If we don't recognize our struggles with the seven deadly sins:

    "pride, greed, lust, envy, gluttony, wrath and sloth"

--no matter how great our authentic greatness may be, we will have blind spots that will impede our progress.

When we can truly see our authentic selves, both good and not-so-good attributes, then we will be in a place to share our best and eliminate the worst…as the old song goes, "Accentuate the positive and illuminate the negative"! Sounds like a good philosophy to me!

Safety first!" This is the clarion call of my dad's construction company in Minneapolis. Without safe working, conditions, habits and environments, there is no use doing the job at all. That's why one must have boundaries—to **"significantly enhance integrity by forming and honoring healthy personal & professional boundaries."** Boundaries keep us safe. Sometimes they are like the little white picket fence we put up, keeping our "yard" private. We can open the gate for those we want to let in, and close it to ward away those we don't.

But at times our boundaries are more substantial. "Forming and honoring healthy boundaries" is one of the more arduous activities we will ever undertake. It takes an intense amount of assertiveness to stand our ground when others are pushing our buttons, or physically impinging on our space. Sometimes the pushback is so great that we cannot withstand the forces of impending pressure or even danger we come across. To some, a boundary set is a boundary to be broken. That's just reality!

Still, to have a "self" is to set boundaries and to attempt to guard them. One boundary I have is to avoid people who tend to "talk over" other people. Either they think what they have to say is so important, or, possibly, they are insecure about forgetting what they are about to say if someone speaks first. Whatever the origin of their bad habit, they are blind to the disrespect and ire they bring about by speaking over the top of someone who has the right of way to express. This behavior provokes an immediate angry response from me when I hear someone talking over another. I may not voice my dismay at the time, but it makes me especially aware that the person displays this negative tendency and lack of boundaries.

The **"ME TOO Movement,"** which, in 2016, began to unmask sexual abuse and sexual harassment against women is the most predominant expression of healthy boundaries of our time, in my opinion. Men who have broken sexual boundaries are being met with credible and sufficient evidence by the abused women and are being called out and held accountable for their destructive behaviors—and they are paying for it! This, to me, is a crucial and explosive example of "enhancing integrity" for the women who are standing up and speaking out for their rights as women, and as human beings, who deserve respect and dignity. Finally, women are being heard and believed, and action is being taken to attempt to right the wrongs that have occurred for so many years. We need healthy boundaries to provide safety and security in every area of every life, in every way!

Service is founded on one key principle—gratitude…"**I thoughtfully express gratitude for goodness received <u>and</u> for undesirables removed or avoided.**" Living a life of service to others takes integrity, energy and character. It also involves time and personal sacrifice. When we give of ourselves to a worthy cause, we reach toward the highest of human achievements—making a difference in another's life, even if in a small way. And *gratitude* is born!

Gratitude is the cure for self-pity and self-centeredness because it offers another our humble thanks for whatever has been given. There is gratitude for (more obviously) what has been given AND gratitude for what has NOT been received—that which is avoided or removed, (more hidden and overlooked). So often we don't realize the burdens others are carrying, and if we did, we would probably show more compassion for them, <u>and</u> be grateful for not having that burden to shoulder ourselves.

True gratitude promotes observation about all that is good in our lives. When we are grateful, we experience the fulfillment of living a life of observing well. We may just give the receiver a spark of light and possibly the boost of affirmation it takes to travel on more effectively. When someone shows gratitude to us, we see our worth and become grateful for the gratitude itself!

In the Catholic Faith tradition, the word "Eucharist," which is the sacrament of *Holy Communion,* means "thanksgiving" and how we are to give thanks for gifts bestowed through the Grace of God. The Eucharist is the Source and Summit of the Catholic experience. The wonderful thing is that it is all about gratitude and hope, present every time the re-enactment of the Last Supper occurs at Mass.

grateful

Oh Lord,
    may that I be grateful~
  it was in Your gratitude that the twelve
 were blessed, and how the two
  walking to Emmaus recognized Your Presence
in the breaking of the bread

      it was gratitude
   that brought me to You
  as my main man
 my true God
   my best friend and confidante
You showed me how to be thankful
  for the "little things"
   necessities of food, shelter, health, well-being,
 relationships and work
  to keep me satisfied and occupied

   I thank You for my life
    my friends, my family—
     it is through You and in You
    that I have my being
     Glory to You, always!

Corsair

Grateful service implies the humility of knowing we can't do it alone, and the confidence that there is a Higher Power who provides the stamina and grace to help us serve fully and unself-consciously. Serving with the gratitude of gifts bestowed upon us creates the fertile soil of human decency and integrity that make us the best people we can become!

This is just a taste of *the RROCKSS CODE* that has unlimited potential when you put it to work for yourself. I wholeheartedly encourage you to personalize it in your own life and explore how it can become a welcomed companion!

REFLECTION 21

Give it away

In a recent Gospel reading, Mark 10:17-30, Jesus confronts a well-off young man, challenging him to give up his riches and give to the poor, then come and follow Him. The theme of the homilist's presentation was "What are you willing to give up?" Time, talent and treasure are the offerings the presenter encouraged us to give up.

But it hit me a very different way. I saw my current emotional and spiritual challenges as ways that I am "poor in spirit," and that our God is on the side of the poor. This delighted me, as I listened to the homily and reversed all of the language about GIVING good things into giving away my struggles, my anger, my fears and my burdens.

Why do we have to give the good in us away—why not give away our bad stuff? When I presented these ideas to my wife, Sandra, she asked a penetrating, vital question: "Whom would you be giving it away TO?" I thought for a moment and replied, "Not to the poor, nor to my neighbor—but to God!"

In the economic world, in the world of business, have you ever heard of people "buying debt"? It's an economic function and reality. *People buying debt*! This financial transaction is an example that furthers my belief that we can give in a holy way by letting go of our difficulties, our lack of character, our pain, and offer it up to Jesus as a sin offering to further our "holiness" (which means to be "set apart"). This will help us grow towards who He really wants us to become. We can be "set apart" from our former selves and led to a new and enriched existence. We can find new hope and resilience, knowing that God has our back, even as we struggle to let go of bad habits. We can acquire the marvelous traits of Jesus as we sluff off the old and welcome the new.

Are there places of suffering in your life that you could GIVE back to God; things you could GIVE up for God; things you could GIVE over to God? Here's one I chose to let go of . . .

checked off the list

when our get-together was the highlight
of my day—even my week or month
I could see that it was just *one more thing*
to check off your list as done—finished
when our time together was one
of the very few times

> I get together with another
>   this bright moment in my week
>   seems only to be a checkmark
>   on your calendar that
>   it's over—done—finished
> when I see you as a friend helping to
> light my way on this good day
>   I feel I'm only a checkmark
>   on the calendar of your life
>   just a checkmark
>   checkmark
>   checkmark

Corsair

I guarantee that you will find a new JOY when you are able to hand over your burdens to the Lord and *seek positive attitudes and actions* that will better yourself and those around you.

In Scripture, the young, rich man asks, "What must I do…?" Jesus replies with what he must <u>not</u> do—kill, commit adultery—<u>and</u> what he must do—GIVE! Jesus mentions how he must give of his riches. I am offering that we give of our poverty (emotional, psychological, spiritual), an alternate way to gain the riches of a clean heart and a gentle soul.

St. Paul speaks of being strong when we are weak. I finally understand this verse! As I show my vulnerability and brokenness, and admit my weaknesses, I can give them over to God—and be made strong—through the experience of Grace! I get it now. I am broken, and because I realize I am broken and the Bible speaks of the poor in spirit being blessed. Jesus loves me in my brokenness, which brings me a new joy—the joy of self-discovery and upliftedness!

Presuming a journey of courage and personal insight, are you up to the challenge?

REFLECTION 22

IMPORTANCE OF PLACE

Everything is PLACE! The PLACE…we make our home, feeling out of place, in a good place with my God.

Atmosphere: for some it is more important than others. My wife's daughter seems to seek place more than substance or material goods. It is the place, the atmosphere she wants to be in, not merely the amenities or pleasures. It is the amenities and pleasures that come along with the place, too—but essentially—*place*.

For many people it is the homeland, the seat of their culture, their clan, their community. Place means more than the land or trees, but a longing to belong and know acceptance and awareness of self. We're all trying to find our place. Some have found it, and I congratulate them for that. Many more, like myself, are seekers, constant journeyers who thrive on the opportunity to, once more, believe they will finally find their place—emotionally, psychologically, spiritually.

Once I heard a friend talk about "his lot in life," his place in life, and it did not sound all that inviting. Think of your place in life right now. Are you where you expected to be? Are you living the life you thought you would be living?

Or are you like me who really doesn't have a plan for what life I'll be living. I mean, I'm not goal-less; I do have dreams and aspirations, but no master plan, and no specific *place* to which I am heading. Is this foolish? Maybe it would be good to have that place in my mind that I am heading towards. This would be a place in itself.

lives

> who would i be if i were totally consistent
> what type of person would be here writing
> if i didn't live separate lives
>
> it's as if my attitudes and moods chameleon
> from red to brown then green to yellow
> environment has the first say

> who would i be if i didn't allow my surroundings
> to affect my life
> would i still be living separate lives

Corsair

Everything is place. The destinations we expect to arrive at, the vehicles we intend to arrive there in, the feelings we expect to have when we get there. Place comes at a cost though, the cost of losing that place, that status, that home, that relationship, that sense of self. But the greater cost is never having a place to lose—never finding that place of suitability, significance and comfort that makes life worth living.

Have you been asked, "What is your favorite place in the world?" Mine?—I am stumped. Could it be Paris, or Hawaii, or Rome? All places I have been to, but my favorite place? I have a friend who goes to the same lake in Colorado and sits on the same rock, for hours, once a year. He has found his place. Some like DC, some New York, some LA, some the Badlands, some the porch facing their own back yard.

Others' place is reading a good book, expressing the self spiritually, or writing something of significance. That place—it's something else, somewhere we have to find for ourselves, and when we find it, we will be at peace.

Everything is place.

REFLECTION 23

ENOUGH!

A strong-willed friend once thought of getting this tattooed on his arm:
I am enough!
    I have enough!
        I've HAD enough!!

I am enough! … feeling inadequacy, discarded—reaching toward significance, seeing one's own value and validity

I have enough! … Sheryl Crow, musical artist, belts out …
"It's not having
what you want—
it's wanting what you've got!"…

I'VE HAD ENOUGH! … finally standing up for yourself and putting your foot down! The stability and power of setting clear boundaries…

ENOUGH IS *ENOUGH*!!!

REFLECTION 24

IF I TOLD YOU

and if i told you i was a teacher
would you believe me?

TEACHER? WHAT VALUE IS THERE IN THAT?
CORRECTING PAPERS AND TELLING KIDS
TO SIT DOWN!

wait a minute   when you were 11-years-old
who did you spend more time with   your mother
or your teachers?

DON'T SIDETRACK ME! HOW MUCH MONEY
DO YOU MAKE?

not much   but what are you going to leave
for this world when you are gone?
        what are you going to pass on?

HEY…I'LL HAVE ALL KINDS OF $$ TO PASS
ON TO MY KIDS!   AND YOU?   NOTHING!
YOU'VE GOT BRAINS ------ YOU COULD
BE OUT THERE MAKING <u>REAL</u> MONEY!

it always seems to come back to money
                                one question . . .
WHAT?

what did Jesus leave when He died?

JESUS?   WHAT DOES HE HAVE TO DO WITH IT?
HE WAS JUST A

teacher

and as teacher   He left <u>Himself</u>   He left the stories
of His life, the stories that transformed lives
He gave knowledge and insight
and hope   He <u>gave</u> Life   He had little
money

GO AHEAD…TAKE THE GARBAGE FROM
THE KIDS   TAKE THE LOW PAY
TAKE THE LONG HOURS
IF THAT'S WHAT YOU SEE AS BEING HAPPY,
YOU CAN HAVE IT!!

(and, if you told me i was a teacher
i would believe it)

Corsair

REFLECTION 25

AND WITH FIRE

There is a line that strikes me in a recent Gospel reading, Luke 3:10-18, where John the Baptist is being questioned about how people would recognize the Christ (Messiah): "He (Jesus) will baptize you with the Holy Spirit and with fire."

John talks about the Holy Spirit long before Jesus told His followers that He would send the Advocate, the Holy Spirit, the Paraclete, to accompany them, to guide them and comfort them. John seemed inspired by these two words, HOLY SPIRIT, to utter truth about the spiritual nature of the calling of God, and seemingly, to prepare people for Jesus' future proclamations.

Then there's the phrase, "(baptized) with fire." For years I thought the fire meant God's wrath, God's pronouncement of hell for those who did not obey His Commandments. Sometimes I think of the fire being the strains and stressors of life pressing down—a fire of worldliness. But in my spiritual searching, it now appears to me that John could have also been speaking of Jesus' fire of LOVE, His zeal, the eternal energy produced by this Love.

From wrath to pressure to love, the latter involving the experience the fire that spreads from person to person as we choose His WAY and give these gifts of Love to those around us.

What do you see in this verse—a fire of wrath, of stress or a fire of Love? How would a "fire of LOVE" show up in your daily living?

What do you do with the fire of stress?

tested by fire

Lord, oh Lord, raise me higher
may I not be tested by fire

tested by water—
    You keep me from drowning
tested by wind—
    the trees sway surrounding

  but give me the Grace
    to live well in this place
      & may I not be tested by fire

<u>Refrain</u>: **tested by fire, tested by fire,**
        may I not be tested by fire

  when my vision's a blur
    and my mind confused
      You see me and act before
        all my patience is used
          (Refrain)

  when I'm suffering too much
    You drive evil away
      You bless me by night
        and protect me by day
          (Refrain)

You give me a way
  to see Your truth again
    I give You my heart
      and I gain a best friend
        (Refrain)

Lord, please give me the Grace
  to live well in this place
      and may I not be tested by fire!

              Corsair

REFLECTION 26

Sign of the Cross

It's amazing how the Sign of the Cross is recognized out in the real world. But how is it interpreted?

It's amazing how the Sign of the Cross is recognized out in the real world. But how is it interpreted?

On a spring afternoon, I was on a rosary walk (a time when I walk my neighborhood as I pray the rosary) and was coming up to my final (out of 10) Hail Mary's—time to cross myself and say a "Glory Be…." I was just crossing a street, at the moment and noticed a young Black man standing across the street from me. But I decided to mark myself with the sign of the cross anyway and not wait to pass him by—in the rhythm of my rosary trek.

So I gave myself the sign of the cross—"in the name of the Father , and the Son, and the Holy Spirit, Amen"—as I passed him. He immediately turned toward me and began to raise his voice, in resistance to my symbolic gesture, I guess. Then he got nasty, and I sensed he was coming towards me, as I began to walk faster and faster—refusing to run.

I truly believe that, at that moment, he may have been taking it racially, or he may have thought I was trying to cast demons out of him, to cleanse him from his street-bound ways, to pray for him with intent to convert. This was my internal observation—immediately.

It just shocked me that such a simple gesture could cause such an explosive response. But perhaps it was, to him, just another case of "shield me from the suspicious Black man" and he had just HAD IT with the distancing treatment. To me, I felt, "imagine, cursing and goin' on about a simple sign of the cross!" Possibly, to him, just one more case of being untrusted by a white man.

But it shows the power of this symbol, and how highly recognizable it is—even if for the incorrect interpretation! To me, the sign of the cross is a symbol of the Trinity, a symbol of LOVE for God and Love of all humankind. If only that young man knew how I envisioned it, he may have not reacted with belligerence but with respect.

sow love

"... where there is hatred, let me sow love ..."

       this
          is
             what I need to do—<u>sow</u> love!

to scatter it abundantly upon all the earth
    not just on the fertile soil
            but on the pathways,
       the ragweed,
       the thistles,
       the rocky passes ...

to shower the love given to me from God
    —not so much as
      to ask for or need
        love in return
            but to toss the seeds of love
        into the whining wind
   allowing the Spirit to guide their descent

to sow is to never know how my love, when shared,
   will affect others ...
      never to know if they
         will ever even recognize this love

only to do so ... powerfully, open-mindedly, diligently

                    Corsair

REFLECTION 27

FULLY HUMAN

*"Christ Jesus, though he was in the form
of God, did not regard equality with God
something to be grasped."*
Philippians 2:6

In the second reading today, Paul speaks of the "incarnational" reality of Jesus—that He was not only fully God, but fully human. Imagine the humility and groundedness Jesus must have possessed to be able to <u>NOT</u> use His power, as the Son of God, to avoid the struggles and un-pleasantries of being human.

"Vulnerability" is the word that comes to mind when I think of how Jesus approached his choice to "not regard equality with God something to be grasped." There must have been times when Jesus experienced the various displeasured of daily living: having a fever or a head ache, or other such maladies. Paul humanizes Jesus, who was like us in all ways but sin.

Paul continues in Philippians with:

*"Rather, he emptied himself, taking the form
of a slave, coming in human likeness; and found
human in appearance, he humbled himself..."*

This is not only comforting, but awakening. It's comforting that Jesus could empathize with each of us—in our struggles, and our joys. And it is awakening that Jesus, as God, could allow Himself to "be us;" to grow, to learn and achieve the skills to create His ministry, and live out His destiny.

Jesus had to live in time, to live day to day, moment into moment, just like us. He took time often to praise and pray to His Father. He used His time wisely, which was one of His traits that made Him most human—just as this is one of our challenges to live a "godly" life.

Like Jesus meeting the two on the road to Emmaus, He meets us where we are, always encouraging us to look beyond our present difficulties and at His promise to be there for us, in personal and refreshing ways, as we seek to find meaning in our lives.

> *"…he humbled himself, becoming obedient*
> *to the point of death, even death on a cross."*

Jesus CHOSE to come to serve, not to be served—yes, He had **choices**—and we find his Godliness in the depth of His humanness. He came for you and me. How do we make OUR choices?

choices

will I run or will I fly
take root, seek shelter or water to swim
see sun set or rise or disappear into lofty cloud?

it takes a keen eye and open ear
to know when the journey calls for change
do I choose safety in numbers
or risk being the lone rider on desert trails?

only God knows which way is best to turn . . .
to sprout . . . to reach . . . to duck . . . or run
God sees the way within me
if only I quiet myself enough to hear
the soothing voice of silence inside

"Fix it, God! Just fix it!" – yells my anxious self
where troubles sit & chum & burn
but I hear God say, "No need to worry –
trust, listen and wait for Me . . ."

so I set aside my ego, will and anxiety
and lay to rest my suffered self
I let go and fall into the open hands of God
and all will be well

Corsair

Jesus calls us to a different WAY when He says that His "yoke is easy and burden is light." He beckons to us to let go of all the constraints and restraints that hold us back from loving one another. He calls us to build healthy habits of giving and caring that bring about His Kingdom here and now on earth.

Habits are stubborn. For good or for ill, they want to stick around. But like the drug addict who is heading in the right direction, building good habits—even the 40% unconscious ones—can be motivated by the love of Christ **who made a habit** of giving up His time, talent, treasure—and LIFE—to show us **the Way**.

REFLECTION 28

Evangelization

Putting away groceries with Shawntia at my mental health respite center job in Milwaukee, I found myself evangelizing for the first time in my life—I mean, really EVANGELIZING! I began talking about inclusivity and the Gospel of John, 10:16, and she had no clue what I was talking about. I recognized this when she asked, "Was Jesus a Jew?" and I decided to share how there are four Gospels: Matthew, Mark, Luke and John, and how there is an Old Testament and a New Testament. I had never given such remedial information to a young adult before. But, obviously, Shawntia was "unchurched," and interested!

What an opportunity to share the *Good News*—like never before—with someone who was hungry to hear something "new" and, hopefully, exciting! She didn't ask any more questions, like I wished she would have, but I felt I was a positive influence in her life at that moment, and that's what counts! Right?

utterances

actually believing that God is <u>within</u> us
such dangerous talk
but 1 Peter 4:11 reads:

**"...whoever preaches, let it be with
the words of God..."**

takes a heck of a lot of spiritual confidence
to live this way, don't you think?
(the reading continues)

**"...whoever serves, let it be with
the strength which God supplies..."**

serving
Jesus was (is) THE ***servant-leader***
and the strength which God supplies
is the very strength that our Lord offers us
each day, in so many ways

this in-dwelling Christ who lives in and through us
in our actions, in our example, in our Christian walk
(1 Peter concludes with…)

***"…so that in all things God may be glorified through Jesus Christ
to whom belong glory and dominion forever and ever, Amen."***

it's the *in all things* that seems most challenging—
in all things . . .
like our suffering, doubt, confusion, anger…even disbelief?
but it says ALL THINGS . . . you mean, God can take in
and make holy and acceptable the very things we are ashamed of,
struggle with and even fail in?
(WOW! God is bigger and more loving than I thought!)

maybe it's through understanding—then believing in—
God's Word
that we can BE Jesus, in our ordinary, every-day lives?
no, we need not cure lepers, give vision
to the blind or feed the 5,000
but to "cure" and "bring sight" and "feed"
with the gifts *we've* been given
(if we'd only recognize them and their healing, assuring power)
then we WOULD BE *bringing glory to God*
in a simple, yet magical way!

Lord, thanks for the inspiration
and for helping us <u>live</u> <u>out</u> Your **utterances**!

Corsair

By the end of our time together, I'm sure Shawntia had heard much more than she had expected to hear. She seemed uplifted, not drained. I was honored to be an instrument of bringing the Good News to her. Funny how you never know when the opportunity may arise. Thank You, God, for the opportunity!

REFLECTION 29

Remnants

Jeremiah 23: 1-6
"I myself will gather the remnant of my flock from all the lands
to which I have driven them and bring them back to their meadows.
There they shall increase and multiply."

On the way to church one morning, I told my wife, Sandra, about how I sometimes avoid curiosity because, in learning new things, I feel the need to write it down and record it and process it and file it and compile it, then share it! How frustrating this can get if I am learning a lot of new, good things!

Then, in Scripture Study before Mass, at 9:20 a.m., I heard Jeremiah speak of the remnant, and we discussed what that meant to us. One group member mentioned how the remnant, in cloth, can be more beautiful than the whole garment, and that a beautiful quilt is made of remnants—throw-aways.

In Mass it coalesced within me…in that, the various small bits of information, insight, passion and understanding that I collect in my life can become a patchwork of significance. Not that I have the big thought, or revelation or emotional thrust. I don't have to know everything to share something significant! But that my many, small personal offerings, these very chards of my life, can become a mosaic that the light of Christ shines through!

Blessing upon blessing!

the greatest feeling

the greatest feeling
is to be a part
of something
much

bigger

than myself

something good
creative
positive
up-lifting

something involving much effort and energy
creating bonds between people and places
transforming me into an
indispensable component
calling out my abilities
exposing my talents

to be a part of bringing
life back to the lives of those beyond this skin exhilarates me
let it happen
let me play a part
a lead among many leads
Lord, give me, this day, my daily bread

my purpose

my identity

Corsair

REFLECTION 30
OIL & VINEGAR

Something to think about . . .

oil & vinegar

                      bustling   clanging
     suburban mall   food court
lotsa flashy colored plastic signs displaying
 possibly delectable entrees
   lotsa skin colors and a rainbow of cultures
        black   white   tan   beige   brown   pink   yellow
   yet (almost) all hanging with their own
  hundreds of people gabbing and laughing
 some (little ones) crying
          and only one mix of the races visible
    two young black guys speaking with
   three young white ladies
maybe middle schoolers--lacking inhibitions?

  this mall, this *everywhere* . . . it's like *vinegar & oil*
     thin layer connecting
        oil rising to the top—no tendency to claim
          that "I'm better, & you're not"
                               (seemingly)
     but still **sep ar a tion**

       obvious apartness as if wearing
      opposing jerseys in a sporting event
     myriad mascots avoiding one another
    not unlike sides having been chosen
   or borders drawn

what will it take to shake up this scene?
blend this oil & vinegar
    in the past it's taken war or athletic competition
        well, we've got both right now

                      and still
          still
  still

        the   mall   is   segregated
who wins in seclusion?

                Corsair

REFLECTION 31

Childlike Faith

"Whoever does not accept the kingdom of God like a child will not enter it." (Mark 10:15)

Recently, when I heard this verse from Mark's Gospel, a seed that had rested untouched inside me, for many years, broke open and sprouted. How many times in my life had I heard, "You need to have the faith of a child"? Plenty of times.

But suddenly, my eyes were opened. It was a turning point in my spiritual life! It became clear to me that my faith had been wavering because I had so many questions, and so few answers. I didn't want to be wrong, but I didn't want others to be wrong either.

CHILDLIKE FAITH—this was all I needed to hear! I didn't have to have all the right answers; I didn't have to know how I felt about all the big issues in life; I was simply called to believe, trust, have *faith*. And, anyway, no matter how astute or learned or spiritually advanced I could be, I would still be far below the depths and heights of God's knowledge (1 Corinthians 1:25—"For the foolishness of God is wiser than human wisdom, and the weakness of God is stronger than human strength.") I saw that I was just an ordinary man with ordinary concerns.

To have the faith of a child is challenging. We take ourselves so seriously. *(By the way, do you know why angels can fly? Because they take themselves so lightly!)* How can we take ourselves less seriously and be more childlike, spiritually? Let go of all the need to have all the answers—to be right all the time—knowing that God "has our back." And back to our childhood we can go, to discover this beauty of faithfulness. Why not seek this childlike faith? It will rescue us from debilitating self-righteousness and subconscious unworthiness,

It will set you free!

REFLECTION 32

"No hurries, no worries"

There's **no worries** (future) and **no worries** (regrets of the past)—choose the **NO REGRETS** & let it all go. Regrets are the cause of true resentments and SHAME.

Shame has surely been a part of my life—all of my life. I have had a hard time reading as long as I can remember. I think part of it is that *regret* keeps me from becoming an excellent reader—regret over all that I have missed in my life by not reading interesting books and magazines and articles. I need to release regret and seek gratitude—that I can read at all.

There are millions and millions of people in this world who <u>cannot read</u>. Illiteracy is rampant, and I dare to complain about "POOR" reading skills? They are actually motivational skills. I actually don't *focus my attention* enough and *find interest* enough and *take time* enough to read well. I seem to have this tape playing in my head that repeats, "You are a slow reader. You will never catch up!" Catch up? Catch up to what?! It is an illusion! Reading all that I could have read if I had taken the time? This is all a mirage, a fog bank stealing my occurrence of enjoyable reading with its lies about "not being enough!"

"NO HURRIES, NO WORRIES!" There is a lesson for all in these four words.

When we settle down and allow our lives to flow along like a river, ("Don't push the river—let it flow by itself," unknown author), we see that all is not lost when we have struggles, that a little persistence will help us make it through—and an occasional glance in God's direction. **No Worries**!

And **No Hurries**—when we slow down a bit, we actually see that we have a lot going for us and that we have more blessings than burdens. Gratitude, yes, this is the antidote to the hurry-sickness of our time. It doesn't even have to be gratitude to God—although this is the supreme way to give thanks. But simply to show gratitude to all the people around us who serve us in any way: the waitress, the garbage collector, the spouse, the pastor, the congresswoman. Gratitude warranted—gratitude appreciated.

So, my solution to "poor reading" is to be grateful that I <u>can</u> <u>read</u> and READ WITH A PASSION, no matter how slowly I go. Take away the anxiety, and "the negative voice," and my skills will improve, and my confidence will come with it. Anxiety be gone! —***NO HURRIES! NO WORRIES!***

the here & now

ruminating in my room
worrying in my roost
stuck on past fears and failures
and future woes and tanglings
it's as though blindness
had become my only sight

then the listener said
"stay in the here & now"
so simple but so hard to do
takes a lot of practice and guts
to stay right here right now
and not be trapped swept off
by past & future imaginings

but I hear the call of an old maxim
"NIATI—Now Is All There Is"
and in this visible plight
I know deep down it is this NOW
that will save me from any "if only"
and every "who would I have been?"
when **no hurries/no worries** *balances me!*

Corsair

REFLECTION 33

WHOEVER BELIEVES

John 11:25—"I am the resurrection and the life. Whoever believes in me, even if he dies, will live and everyone who lives and believes in me will never die."

It almost sounds like Jesus is talking in a circle, but He really isn't. He is emphasizing the spiritual reality that He is the answer to our woes and struggles.

In the Gospel, Martha, the sister of Lazarus who had died four days earlier, says "Yes, Lord, I have come to believe that you are the Christ, the Son of God, the one coming into the world." But it seems Martha had doubts if Jesus would do anything for her deceased brother. Martha's doubt was squashed when Jesus raised Lazarus from the dead. Sometimes our beliefs just need a little practical urging to help us truly believe.

A friend of mine, Janice, was the beneficiary of her family's prayers which were answered when her breast cancer was miraculously cured—assisted by hundreds of prayers and good thoughts. Those who prayed for her were bolstered in their faith, knowing that their prayers had been answered affirmatively. A longer life on earth—riches in Heaven. Jesus truly is the Resurrection and the Life!

Yet, thanks to human nature, often we still have doubts…

Misbelief

un   unsu
        un   sur

            u s ure
            n

    unsure   e

fear dances
            sorrow smiling

inferiorincapableunstablebrokeninhibited

in the darkness

        blackout

    shadow walk

                      gray areas

angerrrrrrrrrrrrrrrrrrrrrrrrrrrrrrrrrrrrrrrrrrrrr

 bottled up

          hidden

                         accumulating

can't cry   emotional padlock   tumblers rusted

  truth of worth evades like trying
to catch a feather, grasping in vain, clutching air

                     self doubt
                      doubt
               d o u b t
          d   o u b t
     d   o   u   b t
d   o   u   b   t

                            Corsair

REFLECTION 34

The REAL Birthday

It's disturbing that Christmas has been over-commercialized through the years. The plethora of over-and-over Christmas songs, the TV ads, the shopping, shopping, shopping—all that have little or nothing to do with the birth of Jesus. This can become very annoying, at least, and absurd and distressing, at worst.

I don't mean to be a downer during this season of joy, but don't these things bother you too? So let's bring the JOY of the Lord back into the season.

Jesus' birth—his natural birth—is celebrated throughout the world as a joyous remembrance. Why? Because we make a big deal out of birthdays! Have you ever had a good friend forget your birthday? Painful! Birthdays—these are the moments of celebration that stand above most every other event during the year.

So, Christmas, Jesus' birthday, is raised above other holidays, not just for commercial gain, but for spiritual significance. Jesus came to earth to save our souls from sin, and this was the forefront of this destiny! Look at His successful and explosive life! So REALLY celebrate Christmas for what it IS—Jesus' birthday—the birth of our spiritual lives, the beginning of true salvific history!

Thank You, God!

Thank You, God!

You TUG on my heart
  You hold up my soul
    You are the God of ALL creation
      Who makes my life whole

You bring in the good times
  You edge in the bad
    You help me see & feel
      I can be happy, not sad

You let me be seen
  In places uncomfortable

You bring me through tough times
   To seek 'soul-food' at Your banquet table

You know me so well
  And help me see me-for-me in You
    You love me with all Your heart
      And joyfully, gratefully, I love You, too!

    early   Corsair

REFLECTION 35

Love is patient

"Where there is hatred, let me sow love…(St. Francis of Assisi)

"**love is patient**, love is kind" (1 Corinthians 13:4)

Every February, we celebrate St. Valentine's Day with flowers, boxes of candy and plenty of red hearts. But in 1 Corinthians 13:4-6, St. Paul speaks also of what love is <u>not</u>: *Love is not jealous, it is not pompous, it is not inflated, love is not rude, it does not seek its own interests, it is not quick-tempered, it does not brood over injury or rejoice over wrongdoing but rejoices in the truth.* Sometimes our best learning comes from studying what NOT TO DO!

Hence, the 10 Commandments...these are the extreme measures of admonishment, with their bold *THOU SHALT NOT*s. But St. Paul brings it into the very core of our behaviors. Who hasn't been jealous from time to time? Who hasn't been quick-tempered or rude? It is through the grace of God that we overcome such moments. And, it is through God's grace that St. Paul is able to capture this litany of tenets to help guide us on our paths to fulfill God's will.

Jesus points to love very simply, in his two great commandments: Love God, and your neighbor as yourself. Either with the **Don't**s of St. Paul or the **Do**s of Jesus, we are called to make wise choices. St. Paul describes love, and Jesus focuses us on it. In the end (as in the beginning), love <u>is</u> the answer!

God is Love!

by Sandra and Rich Melcher
All Saints Catholic Church

REFLECTION 36

Jesus & me

Sometimes, constructive revere can boost the imagination into new heights. Below is blessed occurrence that "happened to me" years ago. It was a journaling experience I had, imagining that I was having a fruitful conversation with Jesus:

Jesus & Me

Me: Good to finally meet you, Jesus!

Jesus: Oh, you've met me many times before.

I have? . . . in "the least of these"?

That and in the brokenness and the outstanding-ness of you!

You seem to always see the good in me, even when I don't seem to have a clue.

It is this inability for you to see the good in yourself that holds you back. It is now impeding you in putting out your "self-esteem" speech; it has hit you in finishing the 1st draft of your next book, Discerning Bipolar Grace—and it is time to let go and see your true value!

How do I do that—when I feel like such a failure so often?

You said it yourself with your many creative acronyms: FOG (Focus On the Good), COLA (Choosing Optimistic Loving Attitudes), D-TIP (Don't Take It Personally), and all these marvelous acronyms. They are

*no joke! They are real, and they will lead the way—
in My name—if you let them.*

<u>What road am I to take—what pathway do you see for me?</u>

*I see you on a journey . . . a journey from self-discovery,
to insight, to acknowledgement, to documentation,
to evaluation, to "edit-ation," to practice and to
presentation . . . This is your path!*

*I see it as a must that you believe in this process and—
no matter the fear or lethargy—that you follow through
on each stage. This is how you are to give—to give back—
to give forward.*

<u>How can I gain the courage to act, Lord?</u>

Small moves, baby steps, little victories…

<u>Hmmmm . . . I'd call it…"**mini-victories**"…</u>

*OK! **Mini-victories** it is … let's go with that one. Make it your
own. Believe in it, for in doing so, you're believing in Me.
Anytime you walk in the light of your own goodness, you're
reflecting Me. Look how I had to believe in Myself to do all
I did—and how My belief in Myself reflected My Father's
goodness! Do you see how this works?*

<u>Yes. If I deny my own goodness, I'm diminishing Yours, right?</u>

Right. You get it now!

<u>And when I put myself down for failing to be as good a reader
as others, or seem to be so, I diminish You.</u>

*Yes. You have come a looooooooooooooooong way to come
to know these things. There's just one thing you need to
give back to Me.*

<u>What? Anything!</u>

Your "reading thing"—

<u>"My reading thing?"</u>

Yes, you know…the shame. The shame of not feeling adequate because you seem to think you have to have read every single thing all others have read, to be OK.

<u>I do not think that…</u>
    Oh yes you do! In your present state, you will never be satisfied unless you can go back and read every textbook, every novel, every article that has passed your way or that you've heard others have enjoyed. ENVY!

    You are wasting your life with imaginings of that which cannot be accomplished, instead of finding mini-victories that YOU are interested in, and pursuing <u>that.</u> When will you be satisfied?

<u>Well, I…</u>

Never! That is unless you come before Me and ask for my hand, feel the nail holes and believe my blood can wash away your "that which I have not read" shame …

<u>Is this possible? Do You do such things? Am I worthy of this Grace?</u>

Yes…Yes…and Yes. As you hear Me right now, I am speaking through your mind, your heart and through these words. The Holy Spirit is upon you, Rich.

    And as your Savior, as your friend, I now forgive you of your sins and free you from your burden to prove, to show off, to fake-like-you-know!

I, Jesus, in the words written in your heart, free you from every burden so you can begin—TODAY—NOW—to live your true calling!

...Incredible! Thank you for this overwhelming and marvelous gift!! ...And, my calling...what is this?

You know...think about it...

...To...**teach**?

Yes, to TEACH!

To teach…..*reading?*"

Yes, reading!! Those who have suffered most, either by the hand of others or by their own self-torture, have the MOST to offer. You have a sensitivity that most others do not have— AND you have the skills to give it to others.

But, look at your new book, Discerning Bipolar Grace, *why are you afraid to look at it?*

I fear that I will find myself to be inauthentic, self-serving and dull!

All garbage! You have a talent—undoubtedly—for expressing what others cannot. You, Rich, are blessed by Me to do all of this, and the teaching is our next adventure. You will go on to be a GREAT teacher, if you follow Me now. You must move in the way of those great words of St. Therese: "I have decided to banish, far away, all fear and all memory of past faults—no trace of dead sins left behind—for in one second, love can burn them to ashes!" St. Therese had it right, and now I ask you to listen and take it to heart.

I do, and I will!
    Yes, Jesus, I hear Your call—in all You have spoken to me today...that I must let go of the reading self-rejection, that I must see my gifts, acknowledge them

<u>and move on to express and perfect them—in Your name—
in mini-victories!</u>

<u>I do believe you have forgiven my sins, and reconciled
me to Yourself—in letting me, just minutes ago, drop my
inferiority over reading struggles and walk on, free!</u>

*Yes. This is so. It <u>is</u> time. It is <u>your TIME!</u> Go on, now,
to discover Me, your mini-victories leading to your multiple
super-successes. You have it <u>all</u> within you. It's time to
come home!*

<u>Thank You, Jesus, for this time of talk and walk and to experience
your affirmation. **You are so wonderful** and have made me so
much more of who I am, and am to be!</u>

*And you're moving toward your fullness, in Me! You will
succeed, in ways you never thought possible. You are
blessed to do <u>MY</u> will, in <u>your</u> areas of interest and expertise.
Go now, and be <u>your best self</u>. I am always with you.
Be not afraid!*

                Love, *Jesus*

(I have now been tutoring an African American young man
in reading for 3 years . . . Jesus has a Way!!)

REFLECTION 37

Getting into the real

One of the curses of bipolar mania is "over-symbolization." This means that, encountering racing thoughts, the mind makes thousands of connections and makes decisions based on random events and assumptions. For me, it often includes building bridges between current events in my life and my religious experiences. One time, I had a grand delusion that I was Joseph, the husband of Mother Mary. Scary stuff! Also, numbers play a big role. I would pick up on random numbers—usually somewhere between 1 and 12—which would help me make up my mind about what I was supposed to do next.

Over-symbolization creates an atmosphere of "everything making so much sense," and it's a time where I have <u>no</u> <u>doubts</u> or uncertainty—<u>or fear</u>! One bipolar trap plays out as "everything means something and nothing and everywhere in between—at the same time!" The thoughts are quick, the responses intense, and the annoyance to my wife huge.

In a recent manic rise to what is called "hypomania" (lower-level mania), the biggest deficit was the lack of what I call "healthy fear." This lack of any type of fear caused me to leave a job abruptly, anger a mentor to the point of her screaming at me, spending money on things I sorta needed, and forcefully confronting my wife, Sandra, on trivial grievances. It was a mess! Also, this lack of fear had me challenging even God, claiming that God made errors in His guiding His people! Wow! How far it goes!

The main agent for bringing me down out of this hypomanic state was encountering numerous unfamiliar factors, such as all the new names, duties, people, keys and work routines of a new job—working as a "certified peer specialist" in mental health residences. A certified peer specialist (CPS) is a person with a mental health diagnosis (such as myself) who works with others who have a mental illness. We are "peers" and as CPSs, we share our experience, strength and hope with those we serve.

This switch from a familiar job to a whole new atmosphere caused a lot of stress, distraction and upheaval that began a process of not-so-slowly bringing me down out of my hypomanic state and "*getting into the real.*" I was brought down quickly, at first. And, week after week, my hypomania was chipped away, until now, when **the real** is definitely the place where I live.

The over-symbolization is gone, the racing thoughts have left the raceway, and I am not spending money on things I don't need. Also, my spiritual life is back in full force, my job situation is being rectified, and my healthy fear is helping me know when to take a risk and when not to. Healthy boundaries are a part of my life again! Bipolar mania did not engulf me once again. I made it through the storm and back onto dry land. Feels good to be back!

a force of blinding darkness

who would believe that many of my deepest
spiritual experiences have come my way
 in the dreary darkness and blinding brightness
  of this traveling companion, bipolar disorder

how could these painful blind & blinding elated times
   be God-filled, you may wonder

      well, I guess it's all in what one considers
            Spiritual
                  I see the spiritual, partly, as . . .
         Whatever helps bring me closer to GOD
         Whatever helps me understand myself better
         Whatever brings me into deeper awarenesses
            of how to love others and myself
         & Whatever motivates me to give others blessings
               that have been given to me

      THIS process my illness has partaken in—
      events not just handed to me
       but soaking me in a rain of blessed possibilities that God
      has helped transform within me into life-changing lessons—
      I thank You God for this illness that has brought
         color and flavor and texture into my life
            along with points of Wisdom and Grace
         I never would have had
            without bipolar influence

            no matter the difficulties, pain and
            lost-ness it has dealt me
             I would never change it
              even if I could—
               it's as much a part of me as
                eye color or DNA
                 guess it would be like taking the tiger
                  out of the wild because it bites—
                   this dark brilliance brings
                    meaning to my existence
                    and grace-filled gifts

into my heart and hands
to give to the world—
could **anything** be
more an ally?

Corsair

REFLECTION 38

Multitasking

Have you ever seen a propeller spin so fast that it appears to be moving backwards?

multitasking

Can we think more than one thought at the same time?

My friend Loretta was observed thinking separate thoughts simultaneously, about schedules and spread sheets and figures; but actually, thoughts so intricately spaced, nanoseconds apart. Yet still thinking only one thought at the same time. This appeared to be "multitasking."

My take on it is that at least one of the tasks must be rote—nearly an unconscious effort—in order for multitasking to occur. One cannot do 2 new and unfamiliar things "at one time" but must have some familiarity with at least one thought stream. Otherwise, the brain would be doing too much "thinking" and not be able to complete however many tasks "at once."

One day, I realized a simple way to see, ironically, that thinking more than one thing at the same time <u>does</u> occur in some instances. I thought of a musical chord: C, E, G—a major chord—each note could be heard distinctly, <u>and</u> the whole chord heard at one time. Multitasking!

From the movie "Forrest Gump," it seems that Forrest could only do "<u>uni</u>-tasking"—thinking one thing at a time. But he focused with such intensity that it made him "brilliant"! Just because someone can multitask does not make them smarter. More skilled, maybe, but not *smarter*. Just look at Forrest!

Sometimes, like the propeller seeming to be spinning backwards because it is moving so quickly, multitaskers can underperform and seem to be moving backwards because they make so many errors in their speediness that they actually waste time.

So, next time you pat yourself on the back for being a multitasker, take a good look at your productivity and your accuracy to be sure your efforts are heading in the RIGHT DIRECTION, or it may be getting you nowhere—fast!

REFLECTION 39

Love one another

Despite the many "exclusive" passages, John's Gospel is thick with language of how we are to love one another. Probably the most familiar is—"No one has greater love than this, to lay down one's life for one's friends;" (John 15:13). It occurs to me that Jesus was not only talking about how He was going to die for us, to save us from our sins. We don't go around dying for others, physically, every day—so what could this mean to us?

Have you ever heard the term "**die to yourself**"? When we give up a bad habit and replace it with a new, good one—we are dying to self. When we choose a more positive attitude where we once displayed a negative one, this is dying to self. When we choose to include someone we dislike in our prayers when we normally would shy away from such a practice—dying to self.

So, expanding this, we may *die for others* once, or even many times, during a single day! To "die for a friend" (or to die for someone who is not necessarily our friend) need not mean literally dying but may include some way they are involved in our dying to ourselves, through the Grace of God. Jesus is so gracious to inspire us in living lives of sacrifice, while emphasizing the utmost importance of LOVE—"This I command you: love one another;" (John 15:17).

> Oh Lord
> send me in a way <u>You</u> want to send me
> where to live & what to do
> all up to You
> this brings me—this life—no success
> or fulfillment
> if it is not <u>Your</u> Way, oh Lord
> let Your Kingdom ride in me like
> a horseman mounted tall on majestic steed
> show me Your way
> the Way of blessing
> the Way of Truth
> let me honor You and feel Your goodness
> inside me
> often unaware as I am of my own beating heart

glance at me
oh Lord
as I travel dusty roads
and bless my steps
as You step inside my shoes
guiding my every step
my every thought
my every *every*

    Lord Jesus, help me know You
in Your leisurely struggle to win my soul
for the Kingdom—
may You always rain in my heart
a thunderstorm of Faith and tolerance
as this kite of my life
battles with the high heavy weather
raw hands tugging tremendously to keep
an altitude of
Love
Thank You, Jesus, for listening to me
on this stormy night

                Corsair

REFLECTION 40

A MULTI-BLESSING

I had prayed before going out cross-country skiing this afternoon to be blessed with the grace to see the gospel choir I sing in in a new way. I belong to a Catholic gospel choir and sing in the base section. I used to be a tenor, but was switched because we had 12 tenors and 2 bases. The bases needed numbers, not necessarily talent. Thing is, my voice range is in between the two—I can't sing the higher tenor notes, nor the lower base notes. So I don't really fit in either section.

While praying *the Transfiguration* on the ski trail, God brought me to that new place.   I was imagining Moses and Elijah standing by Jesus, blazing in white, but wondered how Peter, James and John could know who they were—since they had never met them. I imagined Moses holding two large stone tablets and Elijah holding a large book—the Old Testament. Then, out of the blue, I came to realize that my choir practices were actually *prayer meetings*. Like seeing Jesus myself in flashy whiteness, I saw the light that I was to praise God at choir practice, and not think of them as practices, or to be consumed by which notes I could hit, or not. I was awakened to see it as worship-time. Funny how God inspires us at the oddest times—skiing! I was transfigured in heart and mind. Choir became a multi-blessing, in the blink of an eye!

This multi-blessing is expressed well in this 2008 poem of mine…

the Fountain of YOU

You, God, are the fountain of my soul
this water that streams so high and free
belongs to You
even though most others see it as
my gifts, my talents, my expression

yet now I know
You're not only the fountain
but the water itself, in the form of my spirit!

and me?
flowing into the form, the height, the force

that Your Spirit sends me
up & down & through & up & out again

what a blessing—what a gift of humility—to see

*that You are the very **essence** of my being*
and as I grasp and realize that I once thought
I was that water simply flowing on my own
or to have the gall to think that I was even the fountain . . . ?

sometimes humility comes only through the recognition
of our insignificance . . . which then points
to our precious indispensability

Corsair

REFLECTION 41

YOU ACT BLACK!

"Mr. Melcher—you act black!"

In 1986, my illness of bipolar disorder confused and misled me with a delusion that *I was a black man,* although I am white. Ironically, recently, in October of 2017, I was inducted into the Knights of Peter Claver (KPC)—a *nearly* exclusively African American Catholic fraternity in which I was encouraged to join.

Looking back, my first job out of college had, 38 years earlier, led me directly into the African American community in Milwaukee, Wisconsin. My personal experiences previously only allowed for minimal contact with Blacks in my lifetime.

I entered Milwaukee, in the fall of 1984, as a Jesuit Volunteer Corps volunteer–"JVC"—(much like the Peace Corps, but serving urban American communities) and was placed at St. Leo's Catholic Grade School, in central city Milwaukee. This grade school had 399 black students, K-8, and one white student! It was a new world for me: the Black English, the movement and inflections, the various skin colors and creative girls' hair dos with the twists, "corn rows" and beads. It was a sociological shock—and a welcomed and exciting one, for me.

After a few months of working with the children, I received my most welcomed and heart-felt compliment (observation) — one of my 5th graders called out to me, *"Mr. Melcher—you act black!"* Guess I was assimilating—possibly too much (?) That was rap music to my ears, and, in my subconscious mind, may have propelled me into my delusion of actually being a black man, in my upcoming breakdown in 1986.

African Mask

    there is
a *never was*
this African mask I hide
deep inside me
learned long ago that the
African mask **reveals**
while the
Western mask *conceals*

African mask "reveals" the inner person...

Western mask "conceals" the inner person...

I've worn *this* half-African/half-Western mask all my life
afraid to fully show others the true me inside,
as I goofed around in school, craving attention
gasping for air, waiting to be discovered
this Western mask of confusing shame & pain & politeness
in the face of deadness & the hopelessness~
my life is a composite, a mosaic of colored
glass shards cracked off my opinions,
my ideas, my hopes and dreams
but now, I stand affirmed and unafraid
to climb this greasy, splintered
ladder of identity
to a new height

I claim
my
Emancipation
freed from the deep dank death of conformity
and courteousness and polite self-deprecation
I only ask my God for one thing…Lord,
to free-up inside me
my true
African Mask
so I can finally begin to live the life, You, Jesus, dreamed
I could live—true identity **revealed**

free from not speaking up when I really need to speak my Truth
free from letting others trample my feelings and opinions
like some forgotten wheat field smothered
by frosty white winter cover
FREE to finally be **ME**
this is my prayer, and my affirmation, this night

thank You, Jesus!

Corsair

I was mentally healthy for 1½ years, after a wonderful and blessed year at St. Leo's, and ½ of the second year I took with the JVC at an integrated high school. My mental health began to waver at that position because it was a start-up high school that had, 1 year earlier, been resurrected from a Milwaukee Archdioceses shutdown. It was started up again by the parents and friends of the students. Therefore, it was very poorly equipped and unprepared for the rigors of high school expectations and performance.

Although I was teaching beloved topics such as public speaking and creative writing, I had few resources, including only one out dated text book, for the speech class, and a malfunctioning projector that did almost nothing but rattle, with few proper visual effects! The instructional films were never seen in their entirety. Working there was a stressful mess.

And it was at this time that I learned, the hard way, that stress and confusion were two of my worst enemies, as I "progressed" in my illness. My system switched into manic-mode in January of 1986, as I went back to the high school for the second semester.

The crisis came to an impasse in early February when I seemingly overstepped my bounds as a teacher and challenged the principal about a student-to-student conflict. The next day I abruptly quit the job and retreated to my room in our JVC community house. After three days of rapid poetic writing and seclusion, my priest friend from St. Leo's gently ushered me off to my first hospitalization. This was the first of six hospitalizations in 1986, and I soon scurried back to my parents' home near Minneapolis, in March, after that first stint in the Milwaukee hospital.

In Minnesota, I had numerous ups and downs, from depression to mania and back again, see-sawing with no apparent provocation. This is where—probably because I missed my life back in Milwaukee with all the Black influences—I began to have the delusion that I was a Black man.

conversion experience?

no

i haven't been converted

black to white
doubt to trust
hate to love
cold to hot
despair to joy
dark to light

cataracts cleared
i now see what
was already
there

wash   clear waters   wash
clean the mud
from my eyes

blind man cried
Jesus! Jesus! Let me SEE!!

Your faith has healed you

now I see "me"

Corsair

And 31 years later, 2017, I became a member of a nearly exclusively African American male Knights of Peter Claver (KPC)—about as close to being a black man as imaginable. Actually, seven men were inducted into the KPC in October of 2017—surprisingly, two whites, two Africans, a Latino and only two African Americans. It seems that the recruiting attempts led this "nearly all-African American" organization to branch out in diversity.

My story has taken many rocking shifts, which led me from Minnesota in 1984 to Milwaukee at St. Leo's; back to Minnesota in 1986—and back to Milwaukee for one more year in 1987. **Then, I left for Minneapolis for 18 years (which broke me clear from the delusion of being a black white man)**, [living in suburban Minneapolis]—then fervently came back to Milwaukee in 2005. I missed the Black Catholic Church traditions and Gospel music, and I missed my friends. I have been here ever since, happily married to a wonderful black woman, Sandra. I have lived a pleasant life, with only two relapses (one major, one minor) with my bipolar, in the past 10 years.

I have hope and enthusiasm that my journey has a purpose; that I am being led and fed in my confidence that I CAN succeed in whatever ventures I choose to take on, and that my experiences in the African American world are irreplaceable and treasured.

Still, at times, I wonder who I would be if I had <u>not</u> chosen to join the JVC and ventured to St. Leo's in 1984. I would be a very different, less vibrant person, and the world be missing the energy of one *black white man!*

REFLECTION 42

THE WOMAN AT THE WELL

John 4:4

Searching and praying and pleading for an answer—longing for months and years, it was there, all along, in the flow of the Scriptures, waiting for me all the time. This gift was in the familiarity of Living Water drawn up by "the woman at the well" (John 4:4). This water that quenches spiritual thirst—ended the draught separating me from "the exclusive Jesus" and the *"Inclusive Jesus."*

In a flash of insight, it became crystal clear that **I am the woman at the well— we all are**—divided, unaware, confused, longing; yet, in the patience of the process, Jesus invites, **includes**, loves us.

Jesus, knowing it was against all customs and traditions, took the risk to ask this Samaritan woman for a drink. She was shocked that a Jew would ask a woman, a Samaritan woman for anything, much less talk to her at all! His request for a drink to soothe His thirst became an offer to her for Him to quench her ultimate thirst for wholeness with eternal Living Water. And she pleaded for a drink!

In this reading, I found that we don't have to prove worthiness. In fact, the less we try to prove it, the worthier we feel. We need to take the leap from cliff to cliff to be *our unique and wonderful selves*—as if we had the confidence of a cougar.

A divine spark, deep within, lights the path we are to take to further our journeys and bond fully with the God of the universe. It is God who brought us here, on this unique adventure, and God who will bring us back home, to full communion, through the voice of the *Spirit*.

Led—for many—by the person of Jesus Christ, it is this personal relationship, in universal Presence, that shepherds us on our paths, with the help of numerous other teachers and healthy persuaders.

So, the Triune God gives us the fourth and fifth dimensions of Grace and Peace (led by Faith, Hope and Love) to fulfill the power of our Presence and an invitation back to the Source when our well runs dry. Here we discover that Living Water, just waiting for us!

REFLECTION 43
Easter Reflections

The joy of it! Jesus conquering death! What more could anyone have given us than three years of passionate proclamation and healing, an excruciating passion and death, and the opportunity for everlasting life, in His Resurrection? To have Jesus engaged IN OUR SUFFERING each day, as we struggle along our paths, loving us, bringing us into <u>His</u> Passion, empathizing with us! These are some of the graces of Jesus Christ.

He freely chose to suffer for us. He did not have to, but He did it anyway…in every way. The Resurrection **_IS_** the pivot-point for our Christian lives on earth. *It is the middle of the beginning of the end*—in time, our end, in movement toward the life of glory in Heaven with Him.

what does Easter mean to me?

Easter means, no matter the mistakes I've made,
no matter how far afield I've drifted, I'm saved
in the blood of the Lamb

it means my Savior lives in everything I see
around me ~ every person, every animal,
every resource

it means nothing else really matters in
the luminous shadow of Jesus, the Holy One

it means the past is washed clean & the now
is set in order, while the future is blessed
beyond all knowing

it means the smiles on the faces
of little children reflect in my heart
as I've become a loving child of God

it means my vision has become clear and my
hearing attuned as I reach out to the world
in and around me

it means I can rest—assured, relaxed,
awakened, revived . . . Jesus can do all that
for me and anyone who minds his Ways

Corsair

REFLECTION 44

The tassel

Mark 6: 56

Why were people so reticent to touch Jesus or just ask Him for healing? A number of times in the Bible it went like this: *Mark 6:56—"(They) begged Him that they might touch only the tassel on His cloak; and as many who touched it were healed."*

Just think, you get THAT CLOSE and not reach out to touch the Source of healing! Was it a matter of respect? Was it humility? Fear? Uneasiness? I tell you, I would have at least tried to get His attention and presented my petition!

How do you "present your petition" these days? Do you go to touch Jesus' tassel with a vague prayer to the Almighty?—or touch His cloak by a minimal request for your needs to be met?—or do you get His attention with words of praise, followed with a fervent request for healing? Don't just go for the tassel! Go for direct communication with Jesus and the relationship will bring blessings beyond all expectations!

Jesus wants you to praise, talk to and ask directly from Him. He values you and wants to hear from you, not to just "touch His tassel," but claim your connectedness and directness with Him, in a manner that He can appreciate.

But either through tassel or touch or talk, He loves you either way and will respond! "Do not be afraid" is repeated some 365 times in the Bible and you need to reach out to your Savior. No need for fear of a man/God who is always there for you.

Yet, if all you can do is *touch His tassel*, by all means, grasp, hold on and know that He is doing a work in you. And He will—for your good!

much more

in the Presence of the TOUCH of Jesus
these words spoke truths
that **we are**
much more than
we have ever imagined ourselves to be

it is in the simple—often trivial—glance at our inner-selves
that we discover the magic of our existence, our passion ~
and what would have happened if we didn't listen
to the glance at the mysterious
or hear the scent of the unspoken textures
that often go unnoticed in the dust of daily living?
they'd be found lost in our own unknowingness

~being and knowing *we **are** much more*~
this is where we belong
in the mix of passionate observance
fighting distant brokenness
and hearing callings we cannot yet decipher,
but feel, none the less

here we are—who knows why—
but in this *here* lies the fact that
the depth of our world's heart yearns to cry out

"We are all much more than we seem!"

Corsair

REFLECTION 45

Freedom From

Modern slavery & racism….inmates fighting California fires for $2/hour, saving state $100,000; is this racism—slavery OK in our society? Why doesn't anyone speak out about this? It's so obvious. How can we buck the systems of the age? In "Dave," (a movie with Kevin Kline about a man who impersonates the President of the United States), the false president says, "You never know what (good) you can do if you just (have the courage to) stand up and decide to try!"

Is this (prisoners fighting fires) an opportunity or exploitation? To me, actually, both—that's why no one is doing anything about it, and "slavery" goes on. What were slaves' economic resources when they were "FREED!" Where do they go; where do they sleep; how do they get the buck? Above is possibly a "worse" slavery, in a way, that still exists 183 years later.

Oh, how the Israelites complained to Moses for bringing them out to the desert to die of hunger and thirst, and how they would have gone back to/with the Egyptians to overcome their "FREEDOM"! How I dislike a day OFF with "nothing TO DO." Have to have a list, even if it just consists of cleaning the garage and reading an article! Freedom can be almost as difficult as slavery, at times. Ironically, so many multiple options that we get confused and overwhelmed, which can lead to overload and eventual stagnation!

But freedom is the bedrock of our society, so we need to take it on with courage, persistence and awareness that ALL people must be free, even those in prison—free in spirit, at least. Two dollars wage—how preposterous!

Freedom From

I've been blessed—blessed inside
with a new beginning
shackles broken in the Freedom From
Freedom From
Freedom From
a life of self-doubt
a life of thinking LACK
a life of NO life

Freedom From
    Freedom From
        the walls of a stifling silence
        an inner-contempt that bemoans
           and regrets
    "that which I have not done"
and "that which I have NOT become <u>because</u> of
    that which I have not done"

Freedom From
    Freedom From
the chains of scarcity that have bound me bloody
  tied me down to concrete blocks
    thrown into frigid deep waters

Freedom From
    Freedom From . . . now becomes
            FREEDOM TO
      Freedom To
        Freedom To be my Best Self
    in a world of my choosing

    Freedom To
  Freedom To
Freedom <u>To See</u> & <u>be free</u> to be my Authentic Self
and THIS ~ I promise to BE!

Corsair

REFLECTION 46

Joy and Peace

In the letter to the Philippians, 4:8, St. Paul shares
about having a healthy mind…

JOY AND PEACE

"Finally, brothers and sisters, whatever is true, whatever is honorable, whatever is just, whatever is pure, whatever is lovely, whatever is gracious, if there is any excellence or if there is anything worthy of praise, <u>think of these things</u>—then the God of peace will be with you!"

Wouldn't it be wonderful to "sail in the same ship" with Paul, as in this reading. *"Have no anxiety at all."* This is a tall order in these days of ubiquitous stressors and tensions. Yet, to have someone to challenge us to have no anxieties, this is a good thing. *"But in everything, by prayer and petition, with thanksgiving, make your requests known to God."* Paul encourages us to live lives of gratitude as we pray for what we want and need. We express gratitude not only for gifts given, but for undesirables taken away.

(RROCKSS CODE #7: I thoughtfully express gratitude
for goodness received <u>and</u> for undesirables
removed or avoided…)

You know, the car accident that nearly happened, the pneumonia avoided, the slip on the wet floor that did not end in a fall—these are moments for gratitude.

How blessed is this for Paul to suggest all of this goodness—to be true, honorable, just, pure, lovely and gracious, and to have us to "THINK OF THESE THINGS"! Do you know how refreshing this is to someone who is struggling with plaguing, undesirable thoughts? Or for one caught in lust or envy, or anxiety—these are a ton of blessed distractions for those who really need it! For the addict, the abused, the forgotten, Paul's suggestion to "think of these things" comes as a breath of cool, fresh air in a musty basement of despair.

Remember, *"…the peace of God that surpasses all understanding will guard your hearts and minds!"* So great to be reminded that God's ways are so far above our ways, as we can easily make a mountain of a grain of sand, and that He's got our backs, forever, in the end.

REFLECTION 47

ANGER!

Anger can be a healthy emotion, allowing us to express
and detoxify the feelings that come with distressful situations:

I AM

I am who I am
what I am
where I am
because of my struggles

SUFFERING

but I don't go back
and thank those
who flung their burdens on me

I don't go back and greet
those who shut me out
and labeled me unacceptable

I don't go back and chum
with the ones who smashed
my free-flowing friendship
on the jagged rocks
of jealousy and envy

I choose only to forgive them and
thank God for giving me
the wisdom and tolerance
to keep travelin' on

Corsair

Or it can be a confusing, stifling emotion that seems to always have us questioning:

What anger

What is
This anger
That boils red
Like a screaming
Teapot inside

If it were
Up to me
I would
Crush every can
In the face of
Pitiful happiness
And slice to pieces
The fruit of
The successful

It's obviously
An anger
Unmentionable
And yet
Inescapable

What anger
What.

Corsair

Sometimes it's just a wonder . . .

Whale

*Anger is a whale
it stays beneath the surface then
suddenly
slides up upon a wave
and blows a spout
seeking an air it longed for for so long
even at times slapping its tail on the water*

*once in a long while lifting itself above the waves
crashing down on water tomb with a mighty splash
yes*

*Anger is a whale
and how do you control a whale?*
How do you tame a mammal so free?

Corsair

Anger can destroy or create, depending on attitude and perspective taken.
We all encounter it…which way will YOU use it?

REFLECTION 48

Beyond the distressing disguise

At times, we have all probably been hidden from our true selves and found ourselves doubting our competency or questioning our motives. But we have champions who believe in us, ready to assist in times of need.

beyond the distressing disguise

reaching toward mask
clutching sunken face inside~
who really lives there?
is it a *me* recognizable
or a *who* unknown to be feared?

some never hear the silent call
to find & know the self
that wants—but knows not how—
to cast down mighty shields
and shed the ancient rusty
armor of mediocrity
while yearning to plummet
the depths within

still wise others find life coached
by an affirming, caring, listening ear
that perceives authentic greatness
behind the mask of tolerant
self-dissatisfaction
and shines a melting light on the cold
drabness of a heart
    unnoticed—
        undiscovered—
            unheralded—
assisting a way for self
    to discover Self beyond imagining

        Corsair

REFLECTION 49

FEEL

Thoughts or feelings…does one rule the other?

feel

you laugh
we laugh
that feelings are
not essential
that thinking is king
& that emotions seem to really
play little role in a healthy life

but what do people say
when they're down with the flu?
("I don't <u>feel</u> so good!")

and what does one say upon
receiving tragic news?
("I <u>feel</u> horrible about what happened!")
do emotions really play second fiddle
to a well-placed thought?

Corsair

…and what about the way we think?

attitude

they say
"it's all in your attitude"
and it's true
<u>we ARE our attitudes</u>

thoughts are our landscape
emotions waving wheat fields
perspective the dancing diamonds off
a cool mountain stream
attitude   so invisible
     so obvious   so indomitable

if you want to "know thyself"
just run off a print-out of your
accumulated attitudes
and your *self* will be
hard-copy evidence

Corsair

It can be a revolving door . . . attitudes create feelings, which create attitudes, which create more feelings, etc., round & round. Fact is, as human beings, both are inevitable and indispensable. Which comes first is hard to tell—and maybe irrelevant. But it's more likely that our feelings tend to override our thought processes, quite often—such as the heavy drinker who KNOWS the drink is killing him but <u>feels</u> compelled to drink anyway.

Maybe, the trick is to balance our emotional selves with our intellectual selves, to produce thoughts-with-feeling and feelings that are enhanced by clear thoughts. One cannot exist without the other!

REFLECTION 50

2 JOURNAL ENTRIES

Journey of an urban teacher's aide,
on the front lines and in the trenches…
two Journal entries explaining the
jitters of a supposed "dream job"…

April 18, 2007

For an idealistic dreamer like me, the reality of becoming a teacher's aide in an urban middle school in Milwaukee, Wisconsin, was supposed to be my ticket to fulfillment—assisting "inner-city" kids in their studies, encouraging and guiding them with the knowledge and skills I had to offer.

It has actually been a *wake-up call* and, at times, a frightening experience. Not necessarily because of possible *physical* harm, but because of imminent psychological, emotional and confrontational testing that emerged on day one of this new job.

For my first three weeks at my new grade school/middle school teacher's aide position, starting in mid-October, 2006, my new supervisor directed me to "float"—giving me no real assignment, other than "covering" for other teachers who had to go to an "IEP" (individual education plan) meeting, where teachers and administrators get together to discuss and plan the future of a student with a learning and/or behavioral disability. I covered for a number of teachers in those early weeks, until I was given the assignment of working with the two 5th grade classes.

I had sought this job as my "Dream Job," a position to expand my skills of working with children. I had six years of experience, some "regular ed." and some "special ed.," and had hoped this could be a position where I could use my talents and experience for professional AND personal growth. I had NO IDEA what direction this "growth" would take me.

This was no "To Sir, With Love," no "Dangerous Minds," no "Mr. Holland's Opus," nor even the recent "Freedom Writers"—all movies of classroom interaction in which I have come to envy these teachers' ability to gain cooperation and command **respect**. I never thought I'd be waking up in cold sweats and experiencing a palpable anxiety that, like this very morning, captured me in fear and dis-ease.

You may say, "How could you fear a bunch of 10-year-olds?" Well, possibly since they're not young adults yet, and they're not little kids, they're stuck in-between. This could be one reason that they are rude, unruly, uncooperative. But the **defiance**, the "in-yo'-face" defiance, is where the job moves from exciting and pleasurable to uncomfortable and down-right scary.

When put in front of a class for a full day, as a "substitute teacher" when a 5th grade teacher is absent (and no qualified sub is available), I am already at the disadvantage of not knowing the curriculum, or the routine or the myriad details that make a class run smoothly. Also, the teacher's union made it very clear that we subs were to introduce NO NEW MATERIAL but just "keep the students in their seats and quiet." Hell, it's impossible for the regular teacher to do that in a normal classroom environment----and we "subs" were supposed to just DO THIS for 7½ hours?!! Pretty stupid, I think—and a bit unrealistic (sarcasm emphasized)! And, when I first started working with the 5th graders, not knowing the students' names, it was like pulling teeth to get their names out of them---being seen as a cop, not a teacher, and that giving their names would bring a possibility for reprimand when they misbehaved. Now that I know the kids pretty well, this is one disadvantage detracted—but the others remain.

When I was a 5th grader, 1973, in a rural Minnesota Catholic grade school, we NEVER talked back, disobeyed a directive, roamed the classroom or hallways at will, or added to a raucous classroom atmosphere when learning was supposed to be going on. This is the "normal" atmosphere, often, in the 5th grade classes, at this urban grade school/middle school, not only when I get the sub job, but often for the regular teachers, as well. It's like herding chickens! Good luck at getting anything constructive done. Yes, I do admit, fear is often present.

April 19, 2007

What does one do when one encounters disorder and chaos? I tend to get the jitters, and idealistic. This idealism began before I got to my current paraprofessional duty. It arose in the summer of 2005, just after I had moved from Minnesota, following an impending divorce. Having been a special education paraprofessional / teacher's aide for five years previously in Minnesota, I began "putting together a *classroom enhancement program*", although I had no education degree and no grade school lead-teaching experience.

I thought, in mid-2005, that I would create a useful "way to be in the classroom" format, that could assist me as I moved toward getting my grade school teacher's certificate. Although I had attempted to get a Minnesota licensure in 1989 and 1994, I thought this was the time and place, in 2005, to try again. It has always come down to "over-activity and stress"; in '89, '95, '05 and even '06, when I decided, (once and for all), that becoming a certified teacher would be too stressful and call too much out of me, I finally qualified the importance of watching my stress level. This is crucial.

Why? It's called **bipolar disorder**. Bipolar is a physiological, hereditary mood disorder which can cause dramatic mood fluctuations—from mania (over-active) to depression, and behavioral disruptions & brain dysfunction. I was diagnosed at age 17, and part of my troubles have been caused by over-stressful times when I have had trouble keeping my emotional balance. Medication complications have also played a huge part in my imbalanced episodes; some call it a mental illness; I sometimes call it a:

"PIPER":
  a **P**hysiological
    Illness that has
      Psychological &
        Emotional
          Ramifications…….it IS a *physiological* illness first, a chemical imbalance.

Mine is controlled by medications that offer me quite a normal life—along with a healthy diet, physical exercise, meaningful relationships and spiritual significance, etc. But stress is a huge destabilizing factor, for me.

I'm glad I finally determined, in 2006, that becoming a grade school teacher would be too stressful—before I entered the formal educational field! I never dreamed that being a teacher's aide would be as difficult as it has been this year. The confrontations, the rude and defiant behavior, the lack of ability to follow simple directions—it has been stressful.

So what was this grand idea—this solution I had proposed in 2005, in my own personal writings? I called it **I.C.Y.: *the Inward Curriculum for You(th)***. Idealistic?—yes. But helpful? I believed so.

I.C.Y. began formulating in my mind in summer 2005 as a grouping of value-oriented words, stories, quotes and concepts. It burned like a flare in the night as I labored to pull together a useful program. The ideas waned when I decided NOT to pursue an education degree at the time. But in December, 2006, the final time I was looking into becoming a grade school teacher, I.C.Y. came alive again. It's been kind of like a volatile stock market, rising and falling, with peaks & valleys, moments of clear vision, then wandering disillusionment.

I.C.Y. The Inward Curriculum for You(th)

by Richard Corsair Melcher

Introduction: *"Fallen Dream Job"*…

~Chapters~

The Optimistic Way
R.R.O.C.K.S.S
It Takes Two
"USA" (Unconditional Self-Acceptance)…
Melch's 9 Meaningful Mottos
"The Brick of Anger"
"The SYMBOL is NOT the thing!":

RESPECTABILITY meets "FBTV"
(From Bullying To Valuing)

"Challenge of the Troubadours"

I never did implement I.C.Y. in any formal educational setting. I have picked parts from it, such as RROCKSS, but most of the other ideas have fallen by the wayside. And that's OK with me. Not every dream can be fulfilled, and I.C.Y., a BIG dream, proved to be too lofty and unmanageable for me.

When I've got a clear purpose, I'm on track, but when my vision is blocked, I can become a boat without a rudder—like many people, I suppose.

Rich Melcher
(end of journal entries)

the tiger without any teeth

teacher leaves the room
    and the teacher's assistant--me
        dreads the reaction
          up in arms
            off the wall
              Mexican jumping beans

    I'm a tiger without any teeth
     my growl goes unnoticed
       my roar distracts momentarily
        with a look of "where did _that_ come from"
         then it's back to noise
          and motion
            and teasing—their favorite game

  it's as if all the bustle and hassle
   that had accumulated inside
     when they were actually quiet and on task
       was stored in a pressure cooker
        and when I take over, it exploded into chaos
       as if every quiet moment had to be balanced
       with equivalent raucousness

and it only escalates until the "real teacher" or administrator
    enters the room in disgust
        the kids see THE TEETH of those who come to save
      recognize the danger
        and cool off

why am I a tiger with no teeth? will I ever
    gain (regain) those pearly whites?

                                and more

    Corsair

REFLECTION 51

SOMETHING CONSTRUCTIVE TO DO

Life Lesson Learned
two terrorizing, kicking, punching, cussing young boys
completely turned a corner that afternoon
when my laptop came out in the *Popeyes* restaurant

"Mister, do you have games on there?"

(games…games…sudden epiphany that
THIS may be how to get kids to learn!)

a miracle unfolded as these two young
African-American boys, hovered around the computer
and soon asked for paper, markers and scissors
to work on their cursive skills
then created snowflake masks with the paper and scissors
which they paraded around the ½ -filled restaurant
proudly showcasing "Mardi Gras masks" held on by stocking caps

 2 giggling boys joyfully marched around
exposing their half-hidden faces to everyone present
an immediate transformation from
quasi-violent-messin'-around-youths
to *creative, playful, fun-loving* kids!
(it's as if the computer's magnetism magically released
"the **KID**" from inside them)

this metamorphosis was extraordinary!
a couple of rowdy, out-of-control, unsupervised boys
turned into two interested, focused, fun-loving students
simply because they were given

    something constructive to do
                              and given a little

      attention, guidance and friendship

(seemingly brought on by the intrigue of a computer screen
 and a little approbation by me)

could it be THAT simple? that effortless? that magical?
if two kids can change so dramatically, so quickly by being given
*"something constructive to do and a little attention,
guidance & friendship,"* could <u>this</u> be a missing link to help a
"problem child" to just become a *KID* again?

                Corsair

REFLECTION 52

Jesus looked at the heart

Jesus looked at the heart. Remember the Bible story of the Pharisees putting their lofty amounts into the treasury, and the poor widow who only put in two small copper coins, worth about one cent. Jesus recognized the hypocrisy and pointed out that the men had given from their surplus, but she, from her poverty. She gave all she had left, to give to the "less fortunate."

Also, Jesus pointed out that the Pharisees were like whitewashed tombs, with every kind of ugliness and filth inside. They spoke lies of piety and power, but their deeds were corrupt and crooked.

The Apostle James, in his second letter, 1:25, wrote:
"But the one who peers into the perfect law of freedom (the perfect law applies to the Old Testament description of the Mosaic [Moses'] law to the gospel of Jesus Christ that brings freedom) *and perseveres,* **and is not a hearer who forgets but a doer who acts,** *such a one shall be blessed in what he does."*

Unlike Protestants who believe that man is saved by Grace alone, Catholics, such as myself, believe that faith without works is meaningless. If we have true faith in God, we will be doing God's work. This is where the *Catholic Social Teachings* stem from—ways to glorify God by upholding the dignity of the human person. I believe THIS is what James was talking about— *"not a hearer who forgets but a doer who acts."*

Putting the two together, though, the being and the doing, I see a part of both in the following poem, as I contemplate my existence and ponder my actions:

be what I be

so concerned about being the clever one
being the open-minded one
being the you-can-count-on-me one

yet I see now that it really isn't so important
what to do but who I am
if the roots are shallow & dried out

no thickness of trunk nor wideness of branch
will bring flavorful fruit

it's now <u>my</u> turn to turn around
and work on the   who   I   am
letting go of the   what   I do

but…
to be a great listener
to be a compassionate contemplative
to be concerned about physical wellness
to be founded in Grace
to be one who truly hears possible reactions
    before speaking
to be a man who is concerned that I
be what I be <u>and</u>
do what I do,
this is the balance I seek

   Corsair

This brings the Pharisees' dilemma of hypocritical action into view, while taking into account the Protestant view of, "by Grace only we are saved." But, as seen in the last paragraph of the poem, they all come together, striking a balance between all parties mentioned and showing a bright amount of spiritual connectedness.

Long live poetry and deep thought!

REFLECTION 53

END MEETS THE BEGINNING

Mark 8:35—"For whoever wishes to save his life will lose it, but whoever loses his life for my sake and that of the gospel will save it."

The Crucifixion/the Resurrection; the end of the storm/the beginning of reconstruction; the final alcoholic drink & falling into despair/and the first step with Alcoholics Anonymous to realize one's powerlessness----all endings that turn out to be new beginnings.

This was the theme of the homily at All Saints recently, and it hit me hard! I saw how the many ways this is true in my life right now: navigating the uncertain waters of a totally new job; leaving behind a valued spiritual direction program after year-two (out of three); putting the cherished ministry of St. Vincent de Paul, All Saints Conference, on hold for the time being; and coming down from a heightened place of energy and peeked awareness (and UN-awareness), with my bipolar disorder (in a state called "hypomania") after two months of blissful, energetic, overactive moods and actions.

The homily reassured me that I was simply going through the process of the proverbial "3-steps forward, 2-steps back." My illness had brought me a long way forward—having the guts and social awareness to land a new and exciting job, having the social acuity to meet and make new friends with more people in a two-month period than I had in the past 2 years—it has been a trip! And a good one, at times.

But there is the inevitable "coming back down the mountain side to reality" that happened to occur on, of all dates, September 11. This was a *God Thing* for me, since one cannot live in and sustain a hypomanic state in the long run. God saw to it to bring me down gently on "my 9/11" by presenting me with 5 big disappointments, each followed by a blessed ending. The endings were beginnings for me. This was the day I let go of St. Vincent de Paul, ended my involvement in the spiritual direction program, and of three other activities, partly because I was involved in too much, and in over my head. Although they were fulfilling activities in my life, something had to give.

Jesus died on the cross (the "ending") and rose on the third day, which was **the beginning** of a New Covenant. It reflects, to me, the Eucharist. As the host is lifted, we are reminded of the Life of Christ (looking at a 3,2,1 progression)—**3** representing the 33 years of His life preparing for this moment of Grace when He would offer Himself up on the cross to save us from our sins; **2** days in limbo, Friday afternoon and Saturday, when He descended to Hell to break open the rusted gates and free the captives from Satan's prison; and **1**, the 1st day of NEW BEGINNING at Easter, the Resurrection, when Jesus, the Christ, started new Life for the world by His rising from the dead, and moving out to evangelize and call us to lives of hope and forgiveness.

You can see how this homily influenced me. It was a truly blessed beginning!

REFLECTION 54

LOOSE CANNON BLUES

Oh, what it takes to be AND STAY healthy! There's a certain sensitivity that goes along with having bipolar, or any other mental illness, especially the stress and confusion. These two factors can put me over the edge of sanity into a place of destructive, miserable living. I have learned that I can take nothing for granted—diet, sleep, exercise, relationships, med compliance, etc. They all roll into a ball of mental health balance that is crucial to staying on the healthy side.

loose cannon blues

saw it in a movie
old sailing ship
cannon fires & jolts back three feet
recoiling to former space & place

but what if the cannon was not tied down?
a **loose cannon** fires and explodes
in rapid reverse
taking out six unsuspecting sailors,
two other cannons
and the whole other side of the ship!
it propels, explosively, out of control, backwards

such is the nature of the **loose cannon**

~in human relations
dangerous...no boundaries, unpredictable,
over-sharing~
perfect image for an out-of-control
manic personality-type that can't stop self
from breaking expected boundaries
of finances, relationships, even traffic laws

the trick is to convert to a
mounted cannon

that knows and follows
healthy, structured boundaries
spending money consciously and wisely,
that knows how to BE around people
and sees the traffic coming but doesn't stays in its lane

the life of a *mounted cannon* is built on
"spontaneous predictability"
where a simple system of taking care of business
is matched with healthy, observant risk-taking
and appropriate conversing with others
in the work place and in social situations
not to mention in more intimate settings

not sharing EVERYTHING
to prove relevance to another
but to share the self
in comfortable, meaningful ways
for both speaker and listener~
this is the **mounted cannon way**
and it has worked wonders in my life
as it can in yours

     Corsair

REFLECTION 55

BUTTERFLY BLIND SPOT

The challenge of finding ourselves . . . and the good in others . . .

butterfly blind spot

since beginning days
butterfly has strained in vain to see its wings
velvet Picasso banners
that defy endless breeze and gust
and risk pummeling hail and deafening downpours

butterfly's inner-image being merely of a wacky
barn-storming crop duster
seemingly lost fluttering frivolously in fields of green
and cities of dangerous wonder
unaware of the gifts on its back
never realizing its beauty and simple grandeur
but merely experiencing *functionality*

butterfly is incomplete because it can only see
what it can <u>do</u> and not the beauty of what it <u>is</u>
not able to twist and experience the brilliance and majesty
that go far beyond flight and into a pageantry of presentation

herein lies the dilemma of ***the butterfly blind spot***
think for a moment . . . . . . how many "butterflies"
have floated in and out of <u>your</u> life unnoticed and unsung?
never informed by you of their
magnificent spectrum banners waving proudly
while you watched and enjoyed
vaguely knowing they couldn't see them for themselves

who are <u>your</u> unkno*wing* butterflies
and what keeps you from sharing
their secrets of hidden winged glory with them
by mirroring it back to them?
an insight that could possibly transform them from half to whole
to more than whole

may I take a moment to describe your wings to you?
would you believe me if I described to you
their intricate wonders?

what lives could we change if we only took a little time
to expose the *butterfly blind spots* of those around us
to help them to become truly <u>free</u>?

Corsair

REFLECTION 56

P.S.

I have been re-writing versions of *the Lord's Prayer—the Our Father*—for over 20 years. It's been shortened, "tightened up," creatively modified—sometimes expanded—and made more personable, over time.

Recently, I felt drawn to pull together some recent reflections on the Our Father, and here is what I was inspired to write.

("What? Who am I to correct & modify & critique <u>THE</u> Our Father, the Lord's Prayer? But I see some oversights and irregularities that could use a little touching up—along with a few insights—so here I go.")

I offer these 10-15 modifications as a testament to the Grace of attempting to glorify God through my creative gifts and informed insights. It is risky ground to tread, trying to change a significant prayer that comes directly from the Bible. But I will take that risk, in hopes that I have given our faith-lives something new to chew on.

Below is the working space for this example, in progress:

**Our Father, who art in Heaven, glory to You
and Your holy name—and <u>thank</u> <u>You</u>
for Your <u>Love</u> in our lives.**

*(Jesus never thanked the Father
in the original version…unlike Him;
"Love" is capitalized for its significance;
the mention of <u>Love</u> brings a personal touch into it)*

**Thy Kingdom come,
Thy will be done, on <u>Earth</u>**

("Earth" is a proper noun—a planet—and needs to be capitalized)

as it is in <u>Heaven</u>

(so too with Heaven…it is a REAL place and needs to be capitalized)

Please give us, this day,

(allowing a courteous tone)

**our daily bread,
and forgive us our debts, <u>as we forgive</u> our debtors**

*(we are forgiven to the
extent that we forgive others…"<u>AS</u> we forgive",*

and lead us <u>through</u> temptation, delivering us from <u>every</u> evil

*(this is the BIG one…why would our loving God EVER
"lead us <u>INTO</u> temptation"—
doesn't that seem just a little odd? But leading us
THROUGH temptation—that seems to fit better)*

**For Thine is the <u>Kingdom</u>, and the power
and the *glory***

*(capitalize Kingdom because it
is a place, and/or a whole state of being)*

now and ever, Amen.

Finished version:

A Modern Our Father

*Our Father,
who art in Heaven,
glory to You, and Your
holy name—and thank You
for Your Love in our lives.
Thy Kingdom come, Thy will be done,
on Earth, as it is in Heaven.
Please give us, this day, our daily bread,
and forgive us our debts, as we forgive our debtors.
And lead us through temptation, delivering us from every evil.
For Thine is the Kingdom, and the power and
the glory, now and forever, Amen.*

Corsair

As I view it, this *new* Our Father may not come to be recited formally by others. Why? Because it may be too unfamiliar. Actually, I will be reciting the original version in all of my public recitations of the Our Father—at Mass and in public spiritual settings. So I am not asking folks to **replace** the original with the *Modern Our Father*, but merely to consider inserting it in private prayer.

Below, I will end with a more free-style version that I wrote years ago, which has its own unique appeal:

Prayer to Our God

Dear God in Heaven,
Holy is Your Presence and Your name!

Please show us Your **WAY**—in front of us and inside us;
and let us know Your idea of holiness and goodness—
displayed here on Earth, as it is in Heaven.

Please feed our hunger and quench our thirst,
body, mind and Spirit
and forgive us for the times we have hurt others,
just as You urge us to forgive others
who have harmed us.

Please put us on the right path
and keep a light above it
so we can find our way~
lead us **through** trouble spots
and protect us from the evil one,
in all the forms in which these evils may exist.

We know You have the power to bring us through,
and that You will enlighten us in Your **Way**—as we stride
toward Your Kingdom in all we say and do.

We Love You, and long for Your Presence—
visible in my life!

Your servant and student . . . Rich (Corsair)

May these prayers, and this book, be a blessing to you as you lift your praises and intentions to the heights of God's Holy Throne. I pray this in the name of the Father, and of the Son, and of the Holy Spirit, amen.

I offer this work of art and passion with all my heart, soul, mind and Spirit, *Corsair,* Rich Melcher.

I offer up my struggles,
JOYS
and concerns
to You, Lord Jesus Christ ~
and ask You to
bring down the blessings ~
just for today.
Amen!

Corsair

REFLECTION 57

P.P.S.

No angel could have said it better!

My Dad just died an hour ago. He was 97. I had heard about his decline only 30 minutes before he passed, and decided to go for a walk and pray my Holy Rosary for him. It's Easter Sunday, sunny and 70 degrees, and, unknowingly, right at the moment of his death, I was praying the Holy Mystery of *the Resurrection*, when Jesus arose from the dead. Multi-appropriate! I visualized an empty tomb and wondered what Jesus was experiencing. Then it occurred to me: when He died, He became FULLY SPIRIT again, no longer to be trapped in a human body, with all of its tedious bodily functions. He was PURE Spirit!

Then I thought of my dad, who was, as far as I knew, near death. I thought, "When he dies, he will go back to pure Spirit—no longer to be bothered by the pains and stresses of earthly life." It was a happy/sad moment for me.

Honestly, I had not been close to my dad for years—not that we weren't getting along, but that we only saw one another once a year, at Thanksgiving, (and maybe a special occasion here or there) and then only for a few hours. Distance in proximity had made us distant in emotional closeness. Phone calls tended to be him merely passing off the phone to Mom, who was the communicator of the household—in my view, at least.

But I always knew that he loved and respected me. I can recall three times in my life when, in front of others, Dad said to me, "Rich, you are the best writer in this family." To be honest, if Mom had said it, it wouldn't have had nearly the PUNCH! I felt so affirmed! And I needed that, every one of those times. No angel could have said it better!

I would like to share with you a story I wrote in a letter to Dad…September 2010:

I want to share a challenge Louise Haye made in chapter three of her book, You Can Heal Your Life. She asked readers to write down all the negative messages we have heard from our parents. It took about ½ an hour to write down a number of messages—spoken and unspoken—that I received from you. But the interesting thing was that the negatives were peppered with positives—from allowing me to fly the Moony one-engine plane, to telling me I was a very good writer, to buying me vehicles, to rearing me with honest values, to reading *A Christmas Carol* to me in 6th grade, and so much more.

But none is more touching and telling than the events of the eve of my going in for shock treatments in September, 1986. This was the scene 24 years ago:

The fine psychiatrist had the family members sitting in a circle...the young man across from him, the father to his left and mother to his right. The night before commencement of electro convulsive therapy (ECT) was often a time of dread and questioning. "Should we do it? What will be the outcome? Will there be lasting side effects? Will it relieve the depression? Is this the best way out?"

As the couple and their son listened to the doctor's explanations, the son was asked if he had any questions. Tears filled his eyes and he opened his mouth as if to speak—or was it to cry aloud—and nothing came out. With locked jaw and tension spread across his face, the young man's confusion and dismay was palpable.

Then, with the ease of a lion rising from the grasses, his father stood and came from his right, kneeled on one knee behind him and put his left arm around his left shoulder to comfort him. Steadied by the loving arm, the young man was utterly shocked by this simple gesture. Yet, it calmed him. It relaxed him. It reassured him. His mouth closed and his head dropped in relief.

The time had come for the young man to re-enter the locked ward where he would hopefully get a good night's sleep before treatment began the next day. The mother, father and son huddled in a circle outside the door of the locked ward, arms folded around one another. Suddenly, the son heard three words come from his father that he couldn't recall ever hearing before. They were actually quite startling:

"I love you."

The irony of the moment...how the anxiety and fear of a stressful moment like this can cause words like these to came out—the words spun around inside the son's head. It was a moment of blessing! A magical moment of Grace!

The surprising thing is that these actions would have more been expected from Mom, who was a confidante of mine, and emotional force of the family.

But God had His Way, in Dad showed a side of himself to me—and Mom—that I had NEVER seen: this tender-hearted, sensitive, appropriately-present, comforting man. Again, an angel couldn't have done it better!!

by *Corsair*, Rich Melcher

Easter Sunday, April 21, 2019

ABOUT THE AUTHOR

As the youngest of nine, growing up in Minnesota in a big ol' Catholic family, author Rich Melcher has a unique perspective about spirituality and the loving Grace of God. Also, having bipolar disorder since age 17, his experiences have lent insight and emotions about what it is like to live with this illness, which can be debilitating, as well as illuminating— exposing the bad and the good of living with bipolar.

In 55 Reflections of a Searching Skeptic, Rich shares 55 of his spiritual writings and memoir about what it's like to live with bipolar, through powerful poetic expression and compelling prose. Also, he expresses his perspective about how he was brought, full force, into the African American experience, through a marvelous marriage and through his Black Catholic worship community. You are bound to find a Reflection or two (or more) that you will find intriguing and be able to share with a loved one.

www.ingramcontent.com/pod-product-compliance
Lightning Source LLC
LaVergne TN
LVHW072125060526
838201LV00071B/4980